Roy,
Let Purpose
win!

Ps. 118:8

Any Way You Slice It

ANY WAY YOU
SLICE IT

Getting to the **Core**
to Discover God's Purpose

Ricardo A. Richardson

DEDICATION

⟨⟩

My late uncle, Fletcher Young, said right before he died that God is a God of purpose, and his statement proved to be truthful. It has shaped my life over the past several years and was the seed planted for this book. I believe that whatever "purpose seed" God has for you is already inside you, it just needs to be revealed and watered. I dedicate this book to the Creator of all purposes, the One who showers us with what we need for our seeds to be watered and to those who influenced my purpose and allowed God to use it to influence their lives. My mother, Carolyn Young, who is an example for me to follow, spoke instructional words for me to hear and labored to provide for me a life built on a solid foundation. To Jermaine, may you discover the true meaning of your life as you journey through its slices to the core. To my beautiful daughter, Raven, who possesses a humble, gentle spirit and who will one day become a woman of purpose, guided by the hand of the Creator; to my wonderful son, Zion, who has a zeal for people and life and who will one day become a man fulfilling God's purpose for his life and the life of others; to my beautiful and spirited daughter, Imani, who has creativity and purpose at a very young age, revealed to her by the Creator. To my loving and supportive wife, Candice, who helps me fulfill my purpose in God daily through her love and prayers: You are a gift from God and the love of my life. To my dear family and friends, thank you for your continual prayers and counsel. To all of you I give my love and gratitude and this book so that you, too, may get to the core to find the true meaning and existence of your lives.

Contents

CONTENTS

ACKNOWLEDGMENT

Thanks to the many people of purpose who made this book possible. Thanks to God, the Creator of all things and the revealer of purpose. Thank you for the inspiration and your loving pursuit. Thanks to childhood friend Derek Wilson for your words of encouragement, prayer, and wisdom during this journey. Thanks to my family and many friends who stood by me and were a source of strength as well as potent examples of purpose revealed. Thanks to Dr. Myles Munroe, my mentor and spiritual "Elizabeth," for the Foreword, forethoughts, and living example of purpose. Thanks to Deborah and Mike for your reviews and comments on the content of this book. Thanks to Clark for your graphic design work. And thanks to Bill and the Deep River Books staff for your dedication and many contributions to the completion of this book.

FOREWORD

⌾⌾

I have come to the conclusion that the two most important questions in life are "Who am I?" and "Why am I here?" These questions are about purpose. If these questions are not answered successfully, then life on planet Earth will be an experiment and an investment in disillusionment and frustration.

This erudite, eloquent, and immensely thought-provoking work by Ricardo Richardson gets to the heart of these nagging human dilemmas of purpose and self-discovery and unveils some of the deepest passions and aspirations of the human heart—the search for the True Identity.

This is indispensable reading for anyone who wants to live life above the norm and fulfill their personal purpose on earth. This is a profound, authoritative work that spans the collective wisdom of the ages and yet breaks new ground in its approach and will possibly become a classic in this and the next generation.

This exceptional work by Ricardo Richardson is one of the most profound, practical, and principle-centered approaches to the subject of purpose and self-discovery I have read in a long time. The author's approach to this timely and critical issue of purpose and self-discovery brings a fresh breath of air that captivates the heart, engages the mind, and inspires the spirit of the reader.

The author's ability to leap over complicated theological and metaphysical jargon and reduce complex theories to simple, practical purpose and self-discovery principles that the least among us can understand is amazing.

This work will challenge the intellectual while embracing the laymen as it dismantles the mysteries of the soul searching of mankind and delivers the profound in simplicity.

Ricardo's approach awakens in the reader the untapped inhibiters that retard our personal self-development, and his antidotes empower us to rise above these self-defeating, self-limiting factors to a life of exploits in spiritual and mental advancement.

Ricardo also integrates into each chapter the time-tested precepts that give each principle a practical application to life, making the entire process people friendly. Every sentence of this book is pregnant with wisdom, and I enjoyed the mind-expanding experience of reading this exciting book. I admonish you to plunge into this ocean of knowledge and watch your life change for the better as you experience the beautiful and transformational discovery of who you are and why you exist…no matter how you slice it!

Dr. Myles Munroe
Pastor, teacher, best-selling author
BFM International
ITWLA
Nassau, Bahamas

Introduction

☙☙

The slices of life that weigh us down—our cares, frustrations, and heavy burdens—can only be lifted from the core, which contains the driving force of our life's purpose. Any way you slice it, your Creator is at the core, and He longs to reveal to you the creative purpose deep within you. This book is a manifestation of that creative purpose given to me as a gift from God, the eternal Creator of all purposes and all things. Winston Churchill is often credited with saying, "You make a living by what you get; you make a life by what you give." My purpose was given and revealed to me, and your purpose is a gift that will be revealed to you over time.

Without knowledge of your God-given purpose, you will end up trying to contrive one for yourself, which may become your greatest frustration. The absence of His direction gives us a false sense of control and leads us to slice our way, sometimes recklessly, through life, hoping to discover why we are here. Purpose is the most powerful force, and it lays dormant, like a sleeping giant, within each of us. It is the force that creates that which was intended to be created. God uses that force to create life, a life more abundant when it operates according to its innate purpose. God wants each of us to have an abundant life, fulfilling both His plan and purpose for us.

The illustrated cover of this book shows the slices of an apple, each containing a section of the core. Those slices represent friends, family, relationships, career, cares, frustrations, fears, desires, and myriad issues. The core of the apple is represented by a heart, which is where the ultimate force of being exists: God's love. It was God's powerful love that caused Him to fulfill the purpose for our existence, deliverance, and salvation. God is at the core of each of our lives, and without the core, each of these issues can individually and collectively exert great pressure and strong, negative influences that cause a lifetime of stress, heartache, and pain. Purpose exists to help ameliorate these problems and issues. In this book, we will journey through the slices of life together, cutting our way to the core, and there we will discover our identity, our purpose, and the meaning of our existence.

Purpose is defined as the object toward which one strives or for which something is created or exists; it can also be defined as a determination and resolve.

This book is about how to get to the core to receive the revelation of one's purpose, and how to exert the power and influence of that force in and through our lives. Both purpose and power come from the Creator; in fact, within the seed of purpose itself waits the power for that purpose to be manifested to its full potential.

The inventor of an electronic device understands the power it possesses and how it should operate. The instruction manual gives the user the know-how to operate the system and, for example, to turn up the volume when needed. This correct functionality of the invention is the exact purpose the inventor had in mind. As we tear through the box that contains the invention, the first thing we see in big, bold letters is "Stop! Please Read Instructions Carefully Before Proceeding." Note the word *carefully*, because if you don't, the very device intended to be useful in your life can be harmful!

Likewise, God invented our purpose and knows how we can have potency, "turning up the volume" in our lives. The moment we begin our life's quest, we each should be given our life's instruction manual, the Holy Bible, with the inscription "Stop! Please Read Instructions Carefully Before Proceeding." In it we will discover wisdom, understanding, knowledge, grace, mercy, and love. As we go through the slices of life—our plans and choices, such as marriage and careers—we should pick up the instruction manual and read it carefully before proceeding.

> &c.
>
> *Rev up your passion for the Lord, and He will reveal your purpose to you.*
>
> &c.

The purpose of a thing is always established by its creator. God is our Creator, He established a purpose in us all, and He connects our purpose with the purposes of others. This is how Christ identified Himself: "I am the way, the truth, and the life."[1] So someone's role may be *instruction*, to point the way as the finger does; another's may be *vision*, to see the way as the eyes do; yet another's may be *teaching*, to profess or speak the way as the mouth does.

The beautiful thing about your body is that your Creator made each part connected and dependent on the other parts. The mouth knows when the eyes have seen trouble ahead or a clear path and declares the way to go. The existence of one is dependent on the other. When a person lacks one of the physical senses, the other senses compensate. A blind person may develop an acute sense of hearing and come to depend on that sense more. Likewise, your purpose may enhance that of the other persons in your life, including those who have not yet uncovered theirs. Often, an instructional word may be what another person needs to find their way and gain strength. So the one who is giving instruction must not take their purpose lightly; their words can have a positive or devastating effect on others. Power exists in your purpose so that you can help others function within the development of their own. The brain is the driving force, connecting all parts of the body to function in unity. It knows when one of our senses is lacking and will assist with compensation from the other senses. So also we are all driven by purpose and connected through this central force. Even when we have a singular purpose, it must be connected through God's universal purpose to function in unity with Him.

What drives God's universal purpose? The answer is simple. Love. Love should be intricately woven, together with purpose, into the fabric of our lives. When you think of God, do you think of Him as a master tailor, intricately weaving one person's purpose to another, using love as His needle? The psalmist says, "For it was you who formed my inward parts; you knit me together in my mother's womb. I praise you, for I am fearfully and wonderfully made. Wonderful are your works; that I know very well. My frame was not hidden from you, when I was being made in secret, intricately woven in the depths of the earth."[2] Picture that image in your mind's eye for a moment: the Creator taking time to weave and bind us together in love. We truly need each other to survive and continue our existence. When one of us is lacking in one area, others should edify and strengthen. A kingdom is not a kingdom without people. No man is an island unto himself. We must function as a team in which everyone has a part to play. God created a community of His people so we can share, grow, and live together. God created us connected to each other, regardless of religion or race. But we will not understand how to maximize or complement the purpose in each other until we understand our own true purpose. Purpose simplifies our complex lives and makes life worth living. It is the internal compass that guides and navigates us through the maze of daily living.

We can become so entangled in our lives and ourselves that we focus on what I call the selfish slices of life—what career pays the most money or garners the most fame, where we should live, what car we should drive—and we box ourselves into this life and then wonder why we are not fulfilled. The reason for this is that we believe happiness exists in what worldly goods we don't have or want more of. In other words, our happiness is contingent on the happenings in our life, and our inadequacies occur when we don't measure up to what others expect of us. Our inadequacies are measured by the stuff we acquire, desperately seeking the approval of others. Instead of focusing on the real value that exists within, we focus on our external value. We believe we are what people see or what others perceive based on what we own. Even though some may want fame, bigger houses, faster cars, important jobs, and bulging bank accounts, others have already achieved such things yet still feel inadequate. Why? Because they focus on the created (the slices) as opposed to the core, the Creator. When we get a bigger house, faster car, important career, and new relationship, we move our focus to the next "must have." There is a false sense of happiness because what we experience in the world is what we base our happiness on, but this is an external, conditional, and dependent existence.

God wants you to focus first on the internal experiences, which come from Him—love, joy, kindness, and those attributes integral to family and community. These attributes are independent of what is going on around you. Your internal experience, like the manifestation of your purpose, is what brings true happiness and joy in life. It is natural to plan your life based on where you work, live, and play, but that should not govern your life. God first wants you to seek Him, to know Him, and to uncover His plans for your life. Only then will you receive wisdom about how to exercise the full potency of your purpose, along with the provision to manifest it. He will mature you in your purpose after it is revealed. God will transform your purpose from a genesis garden experience to a revelation experience.

Your life did not begin at the time of your birth, but at the time God established a purpose for you. This purpose existed before you even were conceived. You were made for a specific purpose ordained by God before you were born, and it is He that manifests it for you in the fullness of time. He is the Creator of everything, including your purpose. Many of us have spent our lives searching to find our purpose in life, because there is an innate belief that if we can only discover our purpose, we will discover lifelong happiness and contentment. This is true; however, we look to the slices of life—wrong people, circumstances, and things—to find our purpose. We look to our parents, spouses, families, friends, careers, and whatever else we believe defines us, instead of looking to our Creator. God is the Potter, and we are His clay, but He tells those of us that believe we have it all figured out, "You turn things upside down, as if the potter were thought to be like the clay! Shall what is formed say to the one who formed it, 'You did not make me'? Can the pot say to the potter, 'You know nothing'?"[3] Looking to creation for our answers instead of the Creator can prove to be the most frustrating thing in life. God knows which spouse, friend, and career is perfect for you and will help you fulfill your true purpose.

Have you ever felt that someone in your life was strangling your dreams? That is because some of those people are not meant to be in your life and share your dreams. How can they be if they don't believe in or support them? You can't change your family, but God will use them to help in your purpose, whether or not they are supportive. We choose our friends and often err, but God is able to use both family and friends to fulfill our purpose as we continually look to Him for revelation and guidance.

The inventor knows the purpose of his invention before he invents it. In other words, he knows what he wants to use it for. God is the Creator and inventor of everything, and He establishes the purpose for His most precious invention, you! He understands that you may need the right spouse or relationships to maximize your purpose, and He is more than able to manifest His other creations to maximize your potential. It is an awesome thing to know that God is the beginning and the end of everything. Revelation says that God is "the Alpha and the Omega, the First and the Last"[4] and, as my Aunt Vivia would say, "everything in between." The writer of Ecclesiastes stated that whatever existed has been named, and what man is has been known. The question is who knows everything? The answer is the omniscient God, the Creator. He alone knows our purpose because He used that purpose as a catalyst to our existence. In order for us to understand what our purpose is, we need to first ask our Creator. We need to understand that without purpose—God's purpose—we are merely wandering sheep without a shepherd.

God's word is living water that nourishes the seed of purpose within each of us and produces faith, favor, and freedom, no matter how we slice it.

Many books have been written on purpose. Some self-help books offer instructions for finding one's purpose in life, often focusing on finding the external purpose by searching creation. They provide a how-to of finding one's purpose by finding one's likes, dislikes, and other issues all centered on self. Our focus need not be on creation or ourselves but on the Creator. God does not isolate any person and their purpose from one another. Each purpose is not only for the benefit of the one holding the purpose, but for others as well. Every purpose is ultimately for the benefit of the kingdom of God. We not only need to seek our purpose from the Creator God, we need to seek how our purpose is to help fulfill the purpose of others.

The Ecclesiastical writer also states, "To every thing there is a season, and a time to every purpose under the heaven."[5] We understand that climatic seasons change naturally, but seasons in our lives change supernaturally. Some have been waiting for a certain season to come, whether it is for healing, blessings, a new relationship, or purpose. There is indeed a time and a purpose for everything, and He who created purpose also created time. God doesn't function by time as man does. He created it; He is outside it and therefore can influence it. But God gave man the ability to influence his own season, too. The only way to do that is through purpose. In other words, life seasons are influenced by your purpose and must change as purpose directs. When you go to the core and your purpose is revealed, your season must change to accommodate the revelation of purpose in your life! This is how potent purpose really is! It doesn't have to wait on a season to exact change in your life!

Our preconceptions and plans to discover why we exist are at best shallow and self-serving, but as we slice into God's fruits of purpose, we discover that at the core lay our purpose, why we exist, and our identity—who we are.

Many of us have experienced frustrations in life in our relationships. These frustrations sometimes come from not knowing who we are and whose we are. Have you ever observed someone who knows who they are? A person of authority often carries himself or herself that way. Likewise does a person of humility. Once you realize that you were created unique, with a specific purpose, you begin to act on it. We know that life has to mean much more than going to work, watching sports, taking care of the home, paying bills, and meeting deadlines. Life should be a beautiful canvas on which God guides and directs us as He paints our purpose, trains us in that purpose, and fulfills our innate longing for meaning.

Any Way You Slice It has been a journey for me in finding my purpose, making decisions outside of my purpose that frustrated my life, and then finally making decisions within my purpose to see life as an opportunity to refine and fulfill a longing in me to understand the meaning of my life. The longing that I have is to see your life filled with purpose, "for the creation waits with eager longing for the revealing of the sons of God."[6] The Creator wants creation to stand up and be counted in making life fulfilling, meaningful, and purposeful.

We must understand that in order to first have our purpose manifested we need to be "in the core," connected to the Creator God. If you stay "in the slices" of life, you will miss what God has called you to do and be influenced by what others call you to do. Those who are searching for the meaning of life outside of God are in the slices, ignoring the core. God not only exists in the core but in the slices as well. Why? To lead you back to the core, back to where you can uncover His revelation. Whenever we receive a revelation of God, He is simply manifesting as much of Himself as we are able to comprehend. He takes pleasure in revealing Himself to those who seek Him and giving them the purpose for which they are searching.

King Solomon, the wise teacher of Ecclesiastes, searched every issue of life. He searched wisdom, work, love, knowledge, folly, oppression, friendliness, respect, riches, poverty, happiness, sorrow, anger, pride, and obedience and found that all is meaningless without purpose. In other words, the only way to have a fulfilling, abundant life is to be centered in God. Outside the core are all the issues we deal with in life each day, all slices of life. We tend to look to each of these issues to find happiness and contentment. Solomon concluded that a life centered on such things is meaningless. Without God, nothing can satisfy, for without God who can eat or find enjoyment? With Him, all life and His good gifts are to be gratefully received and used and enjoyed to the fullest. "To the man who pleases Him, God gives wisdom, knowledge, and happiness, but to the one who displeases him, He gives the task of gathering and storing up wealth to hand it over to the one who pleases God."[7] Again, God is the one who gives wisdom, knowledge, and happiness. It seems to me that the One who has these gifts knows the purpose of life. It is only through knowing true purpose that you can have wisdom and happiness. The teacher concludes that we discover the purpose in life if we first "fear God and keep his commandments, for this is the duty of all mankind."[8]

This book is about fulfilling that duty, receiving a manifestation of your purpose, and learning to live your life in the core of God's purpose.

Chapter One
A Relentless Pursuit

☙❧

The pupose in a man's heart is like deep water, but a man of understanding will draw it out.

PROVERBS 20:5 ESV

Many of us have wanted something so badly that we would do whatever it took to get it. We would have a relentless attitude to not give up or be defeated until we got what we desired. I remember how badly I wanted a new bicycle when I was a young boy. Not just any bicycle but a Huffy with a banana seat (or as young Bahamians would say, "a loaf of bread seat"). No one in my neighborhood had a bicycle with a long, soft seat, and I was determined to be the first. I knew that if I got that bicycle all the other kids would see me as the cool, popular, admired person I was destined, in my mind, to be. I remember doing whatever my mother asked; I was on my best behavior for almost a year. I worked hard to get better grades, tried to stay out of trouble, and did all the things around the house she asked me to do. I had a goal, and my attitude and character were shaped by that goal. I was relentless in my pursuit of that soft, cushioned-seat bicycle, and nothing or no one would stand in my way.

Most of us have this same relentless pursuit for our existence in life. We get to a point where we question ourselves about the real fulfillment and meaning of life. There must be more to life than this. What am I here for? How can I make a difference? How will I be remembered when I'm gone? These questions are echoed even more frequently as we get older and start to realize that the tangible things and stuff we have been pursuing all our lives do not hold the key to happiness and fulfillment. The way we pursued the goals, aspirations, wealth, relationships, and other created substances is the same way we try to pursue purpose. We spend our lives, money, time, and effort relentlessly pursuing purpose through creation only to have it elude us. That is because we have the wrong approach. If you read the book of Proverbs, you see that Wisdom is calling out to anyone who will listen. Your purpose is the same. God has programmed purpose to pursue you as you pursue Him. It lies dormant in the core of your being and can only be activated by the One who put it there!

When you earnestly seek God, He gives you purpose, wisdom, knowledge, and happiness. But if you pursue creation, you will come up short. In other words, just as God will manifest His purpose in your life when you search for Him, He has programmed purpose to pursue you once it is revealed. He will give you the plans and desires you need, and you will discover a longing fulfilled when His purpose pursues you. The closer you are to the core, your Creator, the closer you will be to your purpose. If you stay in the slices, you will be frustrated about the existence of your life. So instead of relentlessly pursuing your purpose, pursue God and let His plans relentlessly pursue you! The word of God says that we should "Seek first the kingdom of God and His righteousness, and all these things shall be added to you."[9] He is referring to all the things we think about: food, water, clothing, riches, health, and the cares of life. But He is also referring to purpose. The blessings of God will be added to your life if you seek and serve Him.

God wants to bless you. His desire is to see His purpose fulfilled in your life and to make His purpose for you complete its work. His immeasurable love is the driving force to create in you a purposeful life, one that is filled with His love and blessings. His desire for you is to not only be blessed, but to be a blessing to all around you. Think of it this way: When you seek creation for answers to life, you become shallow, like a saucer, but when you seek the Creator, you become like a cup that can be filled! God wants to fill your cup so that it overflows. Then all the other people (or saucers) in your life will also be filled and will one day look to the Creator to turn their shallow lives into something deep and meaningful. As you support others in their pursuit to find a meaningful relationship with the Creator, you act as a cup in their life, and as they are blessed, you are blessed. Likewise, those who pray and support you in having a meaningful relationship with God will also be blessed as you are blessed. The Bible tells an amazing story about His purpose pursuing us and His blessings overtaking us. The story is about Joseph, the prince of Egypt.[10]

Joseph was one of the twelve sons of Jacob, also known as Israel. Joseph and his younger brother, Benjamin, were born of Rachel, who was Israel's favorite wife. Israel loved Joseph because he was born to him in his old age and was Rachel's son. He loved Joseph so much that he made a beautiful, richly ornamented, colorful robe for him. When his brothers saw Joseph in the coat, they hated him and could not speak any kind words to him. They hated only what they could see in his outer appearance but could not see his true purpose, which lay deep within him. The story points out in the very beginning that Joseph was a dreamer. The Bible shows that God often speaks in dreams, so the fact that Joseph was a dreamer indicates that he had a close relationship with God. One day Joseph had a dream, which was God manifesting Joseph's purpose in life. Joseph told his brothers that in his dream they were all binding sheaves of grain out in the field when suddenly his sheave rose and stood upright, while his brothers' sheaves gathered around his and bowed down to it. Of course this angered the brothers, and they protested to him that he would not rule over them and they would never bow down to him. Let me point out here that the brothers were visibly upset with Joseph for his dream, but there was a deeper issue about his purpose that would drive them from anger to hate. They were focusing on the slices of his life, but Joseph kept dreaming; he stayed in the core, connected to God. As his brothers stayed shallow in their relationship with Joseph, he stayed deep in his relationship with God. As he kept sharing the deeper meaning of his dream, something was stirred up in his family.

Joseph had another dream and shared it with Israel. In this dream, the sun, moon, and eleven stars bowed down to him. His father rebuked him saying, "What is this dream that you have dreamed? Shall your mother and I and your brothers indeed come to bow down to the earth before you?"[11] After hearing of this dream, his brothers hated him even more and plotted how they would destroy him.

Joseph did what you and I do every day. He looked to his father, brothers, and family to help define his purpose. He shared his purpose with them through his dream for them to celebrate with him, first to his brothers, then to his father. God was the one who manifested His purpose to him, yet Joseph told his family. He looked to creation instead of the Creator. He would later discover that sometimes those in creation want to harm your dream and cancel your purpose, but God uses creation to birth our purpose whether creation intends to harm it or not. I am so thankful it is not up to creation but the Creator!

As I mentioned earlier, once revealed by God, purpose will relentlessly pursue you. Joseph's purpose was slowly being manifested to him, and it would continue to pursue him until fully realized. The story goes on to tell how Joseph's father, Israel, sent him to check on his brothers while they were in the field, not aware that his sons were intending to kill Joseph.

Joseph went from the Valley of Hebron to meet his brothers in Shechem. Already his purpose is symbolically taking him to physically higher ground in Shechem where his brothers were. He finds his brothers in the field, and when they see him in the distance, they ridicule him as a dreamer and plot to kill him. Truthfully, they hated Joseph's purpose more than they hated Joseph. Had Joseph never shared his dream with his brothers they may have spared him. I believe that his brothers were afraid of what Joseph would become. Had he not threatened them, they would have left Joseph and his dreams alone. But they meant to harm him because in their minds, if they did, he would never rule over them. They threw him into a cistern and discussed how they would destroy him. After debating among them, Judah, the oldest brother, pleaded to spare Joseph's life. Out of all his brothers, the one whose name means "praise" saved Joseph's life. When we go through trials in life, it is often our praise to God that saves our purpose from destruction. The brothers honored Judah and decided to sell him to some Ishmaelites who were traveling to Egypt.

Notice that all of their thoughts were geared toward a selfish end, to rid themselves of Joseph and temporarily enrich their lives. Money was a motivating factor as well as pride, jealousy, hatred, and selfishness. Have you ever made a decision that was motivated by money, jealousy, selfishness, or pride? There is usually no long-term gain when we make decisions based on these factors.

Genesis 37 records that the brothers took Joseph's robe, dipped it in animal blood, and told their father that he had been torn to pieces by some ferocious beast. Israel believed them and mourned his beloved son's death, not realizing that the ferociousness had come from his own sons.

Meanwhile, Joseph was taken to Egypt and sold to Potiphar, one of Pharaoh's officials and the captain of the guard. The Lord was with Joseph and he prospered while living in the house of his Egyptian master. The Lord's purpose was evident in Joseph's life, and Potiphar recognized it. When Potiphar saw that the Lord was with him and that the Lord gave him success in everything he did, Joseph found favor in his master's eyes and became his attendant. Potiphar was shrewd and promoted Joseph for selfish reasons because of God's favor on his life. He knew that he would receive blessings as Joseph was blessed. Potiphar put him in charge of his household and entrusted to his care everything he owned. From the time he put Joseph in charge, the Lord blessed the household of the Egyptian.

Metaphorically, Joseph's life was in the core and Potiphar's was in the slices, but because he stayed connected to Joseph, everything Potiphar had—house and field—was blessed. So he left all in Joseph's charge and did not concern himself with anything of importance.

Joseph's season had not yet come to fulfill his purpose, but his purpose was opening the doors for blessings from God, even as it was pursuing him. As purpose pursues you, so do blessings and success on every level. In fact, as Joseph got closer to his purpose, his blessings and successes increased. The potency of your purpose is measured by both your life and the lives around you that it affects. The provisions and blessings of God are in direct proportion to the potency of your purpose. The more potent the purpose becomes, the more abundant the blessings, but these blessings sometimes come with trials and persecutions. When you operate in your purpose, the blessings will overtake you. As God promoted Joseph, man tried to demote him. He was accused of assaulting Potiphar's wife and imprisoned unjustly, yet the warden put him in charge of all the prisoners. Joseph's purpose was becoming so potent that no matter where he went he received favor, even in jail.

While blessings followed Joseph in Potiphar's house and in prison, his purpose was to be fulfilled in the house of Pharaoh. The trials with Potiphar and his wife were a testing from God of Joseph's preparedness to complete His divine purpose. Likewise, we will be tested in this life as well through family, friends, and work, even our spouse.

Some of you may be going through some prison experiences, too, but they are only to prepare you for your palace experiences, where blessings abound. What God had in store for Joseph was above all he could imagine or think; he could only dream it. God intended Joseph to be governor of Egypt, and even Potiphar would have to answer to him. He would become the head of the king's household and second-in-command of the entire kingdom.

Some time later, the king's cupbearer and baker offended Pharaoh, who had them imprisoned with Joseph. They both had strange dreams, and Joseph told them that the God he served could interpret them. Joseph was so centered in the core that he gave God glory even after being confined by prison walls. He informed the cupbearer that he would be restored to the service of Pharaoh but the baker would be hanged within three days' time. Joseph asked the cupbearer to remember him when he was restored and to mention him to Pharaoh because he had been unjustly imprisoned. Within three days, just as Joseph had prophesied, Pharaoh restored the cupbearer to his position, but the cupbearer forgot Joseph. Again, Joseph had looked to the created for deliverance instead of the Creator.

Joseph remained in prison for two more years, patiently waiting on God. I believe that during that time Joseph focused on getting deeper in the core and came to trust God alone for his deliverance. He was going through a prison experience that showed him who he was and, more importantly, who God was. This is a valuable lesson for all to learn. Joseph praised God in his prison experience and trusted Him to promote him to a palace experience.

After two full years (730 days) had passed, the Bible says Pharaoh had a dream. He was standing by the Nile when out of the river came seven cows, sleek and fat, and they grazed among the reeds. After them, seven other cows, ugly and gaunt, came up out of the Nile and ate up the seven sleek, fat cows. He had a second dream where seven heads of grain, healthy and good, grew on a single stalk. After them, seven other heads of grain, thin and scorched by the east wind, sprouted and swallowed up the seven healthy heads. Pharaoh was troubled in his mind and sent for all the magicians and wise men of Egypt, but none could interpret the dreams. Then the cupbearer remembered Joseph and told Pharaoh how he had interpreted his dream while in prison.

Remember, Joseph had asked the cupbearer to give a good report to Pharaoh after his restoration period, but the cupbearer did not mentioned a word of Joseph until 730 days later, and then only told of Joseph to show himself of value to Pharaoh. Oftentimes creation is only concerned about itself. During the 730-day period of the cupbearer's amnesia, Joseph's relationship with and dependence on God grew. It is often during times of imprisonment and distress that we reflect deeply on our lives, reaching deep within to our core to get the answers for which we are searching. In these times in which we live, we cannot depend on man or creation for our answers and deliverance. Although we may not be in a physical prison as was Joseph, we often find ourselves imprisoned by fear and uncertainty. At this weakest point in our lives, God's purpose for us is strengthened, as God's strength is made perfect in our weakness. In the solemnity of prison, Joseph trusted that God would deliver him because his purpose had not yet been manifested.

In continuing Joseph's account, Pharaoh summoned him to interpret the dreams. Joseph told Pharaoh that he could not tell him his dream but that God would. He acknowledged God and gave Him the glory, which is evidence of his deep relationship with the Father. Joseph explained that the seven fat cows and healthy heads of grains in Pharaoh's dreams represent seven years of abundance, and the seven ugly cows and grain represent seven years of severe famine that would come upon the land. He wisely advised Pharaoh to store up the grain in the years of abundance so that food would be available during the famine. Joseph was the only true wise man in Pharaoh's eyes because he had already searched for other men to interpret his dream. While Joseph was locked away and meditating on God and his purpose, God had already reduced the wise men in Pharaoh's court, not giving anyone else the interpretation of the king's dream. Joseph's purpose was making room for him to be in the presence of the King. Pharaoh then appointed Joseph as governor of the land and decreed there was to be no one higher than he, and only with respect to the throne would Pharaoh be greater than Joseph. He was now second-in-command in Pharaoh's presence and chief commander in Pharaoh's absence.

Joseph's purpose was becoming more potent, as were his blessings and his responsibilities. The people affected by his purpose would measure the potency of his purpose. Joseph's purpose was to deliver Egypt from famine and ultimately save his own people. He was now operating in the purpose that God had designed for him. He stored up all the grain from the years of plenty, so only Egypt had food during the severe famine. Joseph's father heard that there was food in Egypt and sent all but his youngest son to buy some. Joseph recognized them when they arrived, but they didn't realize he was their forsaken brother. Immediately when they saw Joseph, they bowed down to him with their faces to the ground. What God had manifested to Joseph in his dreams as a young boy had been realized. His purpose, to save the people of the land, including his own family and brothers, was now being fulfilled.

Have you ever told another person that they were naturally talented in something? Others may refer to it as a gift. I heard a sixteen-year-old girl in my church sing, and there is no doubt that she has a gifted voice. "That girl can sing!" someone shouted. Indeed, your purpose will begin to reveal itself through your gifts, because that is exactly what purpose is: a gift from your Creator! You will find that your gift will open doors for your purpose to be fulfilled. So it was true for Joseph, whose gift was dreaming and the interpretation of dreams. This gift made room and opened the door before the king of Egypt so that his purpose could walk in. So don't stop at your gift; ask God to take you deeper, to the core, where love and purpose live.

The story tells us that Joseph's younger brother and father finally come to Egypt, and they all bow down before Joseph. When Joseph reveals himself to his family, he tells them that they should not be angry or distressed because it was God who sent him to Egypt ahead of them to save their lives.

God used this famine in Egypt as a backdrop to illuminate Joseph's purpose and gift. Joseph understood that when you operate in the Creator's will, even imminent devastation from a famine can be used for good. This Biblical famine drove his brothers to their knees, literally. They bowed before Joseph as he had dreamed they would. They realized that Joseph held their lives in the balance and had the power to save them or allow the famine to destroy them. This was his purpose. I wonder how many of us would be willing to endure the suffering that Joseph experienced. Remember, God gave Joseph the dream of all bowing before him but not the hardship that would come before. In other words, he showed Joseph the palace, not the prison. Many of us can relate to this. We see the promise but not the process, which often comes with persecution. Joseph understood that his purpose made room for him in Pharaoh's kingdom. He also recognized that God allowed events in his life to happen to bring him to such a position. People who believe their accomplishments are by their own design don't understand the purpose and plan of God. Joseph was able to show compassion to those who tried to harm him because he knew that they didn't realize what they were doing when they plotted to destroy his life. Jesus showed the same compassion on the cross at Calvary when he said, "Father, forgive them, for they do not know what they do."[12]

Purpose is a gift not to be pursued or achieved, but one that must be received. The purpose of one's life is like a parable hidden in created man that can only be explained or revealed by God, the Creator of man.

This story of Joseph's life teaches us so much about God, His kingdom, and His purpose. Joseph's father, Israel, would become a nation known by his name, and it was Joseph's purpose that preserved this nation. However, the people would not operate in the purpose God intended for them so He raised up nations against them. God is sovereign; nothing happens without His knowledge and/or approval. As stated earlier, God either allows or arranges for everything to happen in our lives. He wants us to act of our free will even if it is not in alignment with His. He either arranges things to happen by His wisdom or allows them to happen by His grace. When we are at the core and operate in God's will, our choices are arranged and influenced by Him, but when we operate outside it, in the slices of creation, our choices are allowed by Him. This is the result of unfathomable love. God wants us to be obedient to Him out of love, not fear.

King Nebuchadnezzar of Babylon was used by God to carry out His purpose against the Jewish people. They had rejected God and His word, so God turned them over to Babylonian rule and dominion. This is a hard thing for many people to grasp, as God operates similarly today against those who reject His son, Jesus Christ. He turns them over to the rule and dominion of unbelieving people and nations. God has used some of the most ruthless leaders to accomplish His purpose. They are used to carry out what God wants to do, and then His grace and mercy delivers those who repent and turn back to Him. Just as Joseph forgave his brothers and father and restored them, so God will forgive and restore those who submit to His will and His purpose.

"And now have I given all these lands into the hand of Nebuchadnezzar the king of Babylon, my servant; and the beast of the field have I given him also to serve him."[13] God explained that not only had He allowed Nebuchadnezzar to rule the Jews, He had arranged it because they would not listen to His word. God also promised that those who would submit to the rule of Nebuchadnezzar would later be delivered by His hand, but those who refused would perish. This is a revealing statement about the potency of purpose. God had a purpose, and it would be carried out on the Jews despite their willingness. You have a choice. You can either allow God's purpose to be revealed in your life by His hand or, like the Israelites, you can have His purpose exacted on your life through the hand of someone less forgiving and merciful.

In life, people will do things to you intentionally to hurt you, but God will use what people do against you, for you—that is, of course, if you are at or on your way to the core. Joseph told his brothers, "You intended to harm me, but God intended it for good to accomplish what is now being done, the saving of many lives."[14] He goes on to say that he would provide for his brothers and their children. His purpose was generational, as it extended to his family and their children. This was the meaning of Joseph's existence. He was a savior to many.

His purpose relentlessly pursued him until it was fulfilled. And throughout that pursuit, God tested him in the process and perfected his purpose so that once fully manifested, it would yield all the fruits and blessings of God. His father and brothers, the cupbearer, Potiphar and his wife, and Pharaoh all played a role as God's purpose intertwined them.

Joseph's life demonstrated what Paul wrote to the Romans, stating, "And we know that in all things God works for the good of those who love him, who have been called according to his purpose."[15] Whose purpose? The sovereign Lord God, our Creator. Paul is very clear about that. It is God's purpose that is important in our lives, not our own. "Many are the plans in a person's heart, but it is the Lord's purpose that prevails."[16] You can plan for what you want in life, but it will only be truly successful if it is in line with God's purpose and His word. So how will you know? By seeking God through His word. You need to let the purpose for your life be revealed to you so that your plans can measure up to it. Solomon affirms this in Proverbs when he states that the purposes of a person's heart are deep waters, but one who has insight draws them out.[17] What God is saying is that He gives each of us a purpose and a meaning for our life, but He puts it so deep in us that it has to be activated. Sometimes we need to go deep within, to the core, because that is where our answers wait.

A famous French naval officer and explorer, Jacques Cousteau, understood that there are secrets of the oceans that can only be discovered at certain depths. He published his first book in 1953 titled *The Silent World*, in which he correctly predicted the echolocation ability of porpoises.[18] He reported that his research vessel, the *Élie Monier*, had been heading to the Straits of Gibraltar when he noticed a pod of porpoises following them. Cousteau changed course a few degrees off the optimal course to the center of the Strait, and the pod followed for a few minutes then diverged toward mid-channel again. It was evident that they knew where the optimal course lay, even if the humans seemingly did not. The scientist who had previously studied these animals had observed them only in shallow waters, not venturing to the depths of the ocean. Cousteau concluded that the cetaceans had something like sonar, which was a relatively new feature on submarines. He was able to discover this fact and many others because he went to the depths of the ocean; in the depths, mysteries are revealed.

That is where God placed your purpose, in the depth of your soul. This knowledge will help you unlock the hidden treasure of purpose within you. Mr.

Cousteau used knowledge to create one of the first innovative deep-sea vessels, which was able to maneuver in places submarines could not. He used his knowledge to develop the tools to go where other humans would not venture. Proverbs says that the man of understanding is the one who is able to draw out his purpose. You can find wisdom and knowledge by seeking the Creator of it. The Bible says that the fear of the Lord is the beginning of wisdom and that whoever asks God for wisdom and knowledge will receive it freely. Purpose pursues you, but you will not be able to operate in purpose unless you get wisdom, knowledge, and understanding of the Creator and go deeper in Him.

God created you and has planned your life, just as He did Joseph's. You are no accident and were not born of chance. Even though your parents might have not planned you, they were only vessels that God used to bring you into His purpose. You were born with love out of God's endless love. You were born exactly the way God planned and in the right body. Your race is no accident. Your language is no accident. Nothing was left to chance. God doesn't operate by chance! Joseph was supposed to be born of Israel and Rachel, a son with eleven brothers. It was not a mistake that his brothers wanted to destroy his dreams, but they did not have the final word on Joseph's life. This is encouraging because even though people plot against us, we can know that God is always in control and is allowing them to act in a way that will not harm us but help us. Everything that happens is either arranged or allowed by God. When you operate in God's will, things that happen in your life are arranged by God and allowed by you; but when you operate in your own plans and outside His will, things that happen in your life are allowed by God and arranged by you.

You do not have to feel sorry for Joseph and wish he had had nicer brothers. God is always in control! You may wish that your family were nicer to you or understood you better, but as God was with Joseph, He will be with you. When you look back on your life, you will see how all the hurts and pains made you a stronger person. Your struggles gave you wisdom and shaped your thinking, attitude, and outlook on life. Your Creator will not give you more than you can handle, but He will give you just enough to shape you to be wonderfully made.

I have observed the life of Michael J. Fox, who was diagnosed more than twenty-three years ago with Parkinson's disease, a degenerative disorder of the central nervous system that often impairs the sufferer's motor skills, speech, and other functions. The disorder has no known cure, impacting everyday people around the world and other famous people like former world heavyweight boxing champion Muhammad Ali, former Attorney General Janet Reno, and most recently, the thirty-eight-year-old former NBA power forward Brian Grant.

Fox was an accomplished actor in Hollywood, known for his television sit-coms and hit movies, but is now celebrated for his purpose: bringing awareness to Parkinson's disease. His foundation has funded more than $176 million in research that can lead to the creation of better Parkinson's treatment.[19] Fox has noted that it was a burden and a shock when he was first diagnosed in 1991. One of his concerns was how the disease would affect his humor, as he'd earned a living making people laugh. *Family Ties* was the original family sitcom that launched Fox's career. He is still very funny and is able to entertain as he did before, but now he has a greater purpose.

Brian Grant was diagnosed with an early form of Parkinson's disease, but said that Fox helped him accept this challenge, and he looks forward to working with the Fox Foundation to fund research and help make people's lives better. It is not the fact that Grant was a premier power forward in the NBA earning a mega-contract for $86 million from the Portland Trailblazers that will establish his legacy. He will be remembered as Michael J. Fox will be remembered, for their committed work to see millions of lives changed through the Fox Parkinson Foundation. This purpose was innate, and their position in life was for this purpose.

The same is said for countless others who take on issues, diseases, or ills of society to make a difference. Fox's story is one of purpose, courage, and determination. Joseph became the governor of Egypt for a specific purpose. Purpose is not for a position in life; rather, a position in life is for your purpose. These individuals had no choice in the purpose for their lives, but the purpose pursued them, and their Creator understood that they would be able to handle this monumental purpose with grace and potency.

All you have to do is seek to serve God and keep His commandments and He will deliver you into your purpose as He delivered Joseph. I agree with the psalmist, "I praise you because I am fearfully and wonderfully made; your works are wonderful, I know that full well."[20] God will perform wonderful works in and through you to affect creation purposefully. You were wonderfully created by God! Let God's purpose relentlessly pursue you and watch Him turn up the power in your life as His purpose overtakes and leads you.

Chapter Two
It Is Provided

&⟋⟍

"For the Lord Almighty has purposed, and who can thwart him? His hand is stretched out, and who can turn it back?"

ISAIAH 14:27

"He causes the grass to grow for the cattle, and herb for the service of man: that he may bring forth food out of the earth; and wine that make glad the heart of man, and oil to make his face to shine, and bread which strengthen man's heart."

PSALM 104:14–15

As we learned in Chapter One, God is the one who reveals or manifests His purpose for you, and He arranges purpose to pursue you relentlessly. All you need to do is go deeper to the core and first pursue a relationship with Him. The question that is often asked about finding one's purpose in life is answered by God himself. Just as God gives His people spiritual gifts like healing, prophecy, knowledge, wisdom, and love, He also gives His purpose for one's life. Unlike the gifts of pastoring, teaching, giving, and healing, purpose, like wisdom, is a gift for everyone. The Bible records, "If any of you lacks wisdom, let him ask of God, who gives to all liberally and without reproach, and it will be given to him."[21] Purpose is hidden deep within us, and those who have wisdom and understanding can draw it out. Your Creator said that He gives wisdom liberally to all who ask. Therefore, with wisdom comes the revelation of your purpose, so seek wisdom. In other words, God is a generous god, and He expects you to ask. When you ask, He does not get angry. When your friend or family asks you for something and you have it, don't you give it freely? Giving is a joy not only to the receiver, but to the giver as well.

Once purpose is revealed, God accelerates it as long as you continue to go deeper in His word. As I've said before, once activated, purpose pursues you until it overtakes you. You cannot escape it or outrun it. As purpose is revealed and pursues you, God gives provision to fulfill your purpose. You cannot get provision without vision. Once your purpose is revealed (vision) and activated, your Creator will give you the provision to live it out.

Do you know that the process of reaping what is sowed—seeded—can be attributed to areas of life other than physical seeds? I am not referring solely to a monetary seed that some pastors and evangelists continually promote, but rather the seeds that we all carry—seeds of love, faith, kindness, all intangible and tangible seeds. The seed is symbolic of the genesis of something. Seeds can be planted to reap joy, happiness, wealth, relationships, and spirituality. Seeds are also planted to reap life. God provides the seed; it is up to us to sow it. Man must exercise faith; for without faith, it is impossible to please God, and He rewards them who diligently seek Him.[22] In order for us to sow we must believe that God will provide what we need. Farmers understand this principle. They do their part in planting seed and let God and nature do their parts. Your purpose is no different. You seek wisdom and use it to dig into the depths of your being to reveal God's hidden purpose. Once you have that "seed of purpose" in your hand, you plant in your life and others and let God use His provision to bring that purpose to pass, to use you in His service for mankind and for His kingdom.

Some of us snack on our seeds because we can't wait for the process to bring the provision. If you snack on your seeds, you can destroy the potential of the provision. In just one seed lies a forest of fruit-bearing trees. In one seed lies a nation. God's seed is His word.[23] And we are born of God's word, from an incorruptible seed.[24] When we believe in His word—His seed—and water it with our faith, it reaps a purpose in our lives. God's word is truth and is more tangible than anything else. His word was what established every created thing around us. We don't breathe and live by our faculties and knowledge alone, but by the word of God.[25] Heaven and earth will pass away before His word does.

Life is real, but so is the word of God. Memorize it. Meditate on it. Let it flow through you as your very blood flows. It will sustain you. Let that sink in your mind and marrow, your flesh and faith, and your soul and senses. God's word is the infallible truth, and your belief in it is what unlocks its power of purpose in your life. When Jesus cursed a fig tree and it withered, he asked his amazed disciples, "Where is your faith?" He was hungry and saw a fig tree whose purpose was to produce figs in its season. When he approached it for fruit, it was bare and didn't fulfill His need because it was "out of season." So Jesus cursed the tree. Why would He do that when it was not the season for figs? The reason was that

Jesus understood that when God expects us to produce fruit from our purpose, our season changes. Once your purpose is revealed and you operate in it, your season must change. Many of us are waiting for our season to come. We are waiting on a new career, new relationship, more money, or better life. We are waiting for our season to change as our Creator is waiting for us to step into the purpose of our lives, so that *then* our season will respond. If you pray and believe that it will happen, it will happen. Life's job is to cast doubt on the word of God, but if you doubt not, shake off the thoughts of fear and uncertainty, and exercise faith (which, by the way, can often be demonstrated in the presence of uncertainty), God will be pleased. Faith, not knowledge, is what pleases God, your Creator.[26] We have to fight to keep our faith, our belief in the Creator, in order to trust that He will reveal our hidden purpose. Paul said to "fight the good fight of faith."[27]

Like you, I have searched for years to find the purpose for my existence. I would find things that made me happy and would find success at some things I did and failure at others, but I still could not find my purpose, that thing that gave me a sense of fulfillment. I have had many failures in life because they were my plans and I was stubborn. Even now, as I write this book, I am experiencing hardships and trials, but this is the time that God wants to use me and you, because when we are weak, then He is strong. Paul experienced weaknesses and was assured by God, who said, "My grace is all you need. My power works best in weakness."[28] I sometimes feel weak and inadequate, but I am encouraged by these words. I never thought that I would be able to write a book. My degree is in mathematics, not literature. I am a numbers person and like to quantify many things in my life. Counting is one of my favorite pastimes. I find myself counting windows, tiles, patterns, and even bricks on a building. So how can I possibly author a book on purpose? Who am I? What qualifications do I have to do this? These are the questions I ask God. All the answers lay in God's purpose for my life. I don't have the ways or means to write and publish this book, but my purpose does. In my mind, the purpose to write *Any Way You Slice It* should be given to someone more qualified in literature, but purpose is no respecter of persons. It equips the possessor to do those things that seem impossible to do. Whenever there is a vision that seems impossible, it usually mean that purpose must be activated in order to achieve that specific vision.

These are all inadequacies that men see, but God sees strength in weakness! Purpose had pursued me all my life and was knocking at my door. It was not until I discovered the truth—that God holds my purpose—that I could dig deeper to the core and find Him and His purpose for me. This simply means that we should have a heart-to-heart with our Creator. Confess to your Creator those things hindering your growth and causing you to struggle. This is not for God's benefit, but for your own. Faith comes by hearing, and you have to hear for yourself those things you need to change. If you listen to something long enough, chances are you will start believing it. When God reveals His purpose for your life, he also gives you the provision to fulfill your purpose.

The Bible tells the story of Esther,[29] who was chosen as queen for a unique purpose not set by man, but by God. The purpose was for God's people to be saved and delivered, which is the universal purpose of man. The Bible also talks about the manifestation of God's sons and daughters to be revealed, which simply means that the sons and daughters already exist; they just need to manifest themselves and operate in their purpose. Similarly, your purpose already exists; it existed before you were created. It just needs to be manifested for you and through you. The purpose for Esther was to operate within the law and allow King Xerxes to provide deliverance, prosperity, position, and power to God's people through his love and devotion for Esther. In fact, many of the people in the kingdom were converted to the beliefs of the Jews because of the fear of the Jews and fear of their God. God will always get the glory, which is the ultimate purpose of our lives. We may get the benefit, but God gets the glory, whether we choose to acknowledge it or not. The prophet Isaiah talks about man being created for the glory of God. God says that "everyone who is called by My name, whom I created for My glory; I have formed him, yes, I have made him."[30]

So we see in the story of Esther the deliverance of God's people according to His plan, and His purpose was for His glory. The background of the story is that Haman, King Xerxes' right-hand man, hated and wanted to annihilate the Jews, but God turned his plan to benefit His purpose. As the proverb teaches, "Many are the plans of a man's heart, but it is the Lord's purpose that prevails."[31] Esther thought she was made queen simply because of her beauty. When warned by her cousin, Mordecai, that the Jews' lives were being threatened and she needed to petition King Xerxes, Esther was afraid and refused to go because the king had not summoned her. The law of the land stated that she could not go into the presence of the king unless summoned or she could be put to death. The only way for her life to be spared was if the king extended his gold scepter. Mordecai's response to Esther's fear was that as a Jew, her life would be in danger of death if she did not go, because the threat was against all the Jews, including her. But more importantly, God would deliver His people another way if she refused, and then she would be in more danger because she'd refused to honor God.

What a perspective! Esther was trained to be queen under the watchful guidance of Mordecai. She was a simple peasant girl whose purpose was manifested to Mordecai from God. He reminded her that the reason for her being queen might be for such a time as this, a time to deliver and save her people. This profound statement by Mordecai to Esther made her realize that she must fulfill her purpose. She then went to the king and orchestrated the salvation of her people, including installing Mordecai as second-in-command of the entire kingdom.

In King Xerxes' kingdom, his wife and her cousin, who were both Jews, influenced the king to do more for their people than any other person during that time. This is an example of God's individual purpose working together for His collective purpose. When God brings people together, it is for a purpose, never by chance. The right spouse or business partner is in your life for a collective purpose. Your purpose can be assisted by others in your life as God intended it to be. In fulfilling her purpose for herself, Esther helped fulfill the purpose for Mordecai, who later became an official ruler in the government. Together, they fulfilled the purpose God had for the salvation of His people. Mordecai's selflessness prepared Esther to be queen, who in turn influenced King Xerxes to install Mordecai as second only to the king himself, similar to the position that Joseph had held. God's purpose was to save His people, and both Esther and Mordecai benefited as they accepted the purpose manifested for their lives. I realized from this story and my own life that the only way to find fulfillment in life is to find fulfillment of purpose.

Pupose revealed yields vision. When a man receives purpose, he receives vision, and God then gives him provision.

God provided everything Esther needed to fulfill her purpose. As an orphan, she was not in the right position to fulfill the purpose God had for her life. Her purpose needed to reposition her. Many of us can fulfill our purpose where we are, but others need to be moved. Esther became queen but did not realize that her position was a result of her purpose. Purpose can make us powerful and influential even if we do not realize that it is being manifested in our lives. Mordecai not only prepared Esther for her purpose but helped her realize it in the face of danger to their relatives. If Esther had refused to fulfill the purpose God had called her to, the imminent result could have been her death. People who refuse God's purpose for their lives may experience spiritual, financial, and emotional death well before physical death occurs. Even if they experience temporary riches, their lives are still left unfulfilled. Life is simplified when we operate in our purpose but is frustrated when we don't.

Had Esther refused to act, she would have remained queen but would have been frustrated and fearful of her life. The fate that awaited Queen Vashti, her predecessor, would have overtaken Esther, and she would not have been able to exert the power of her position. On the other hand, Mordecai's purpose was to assist Esther in delivering their people. Esther was an orphan, and Mordecai had taken her in. He'd groomed her and prepared her to be queen. He believed she could become queen and imparted that belief to her. A lesson here is you still need to dream, have aspirations and goals, and work hard to achieve them, even if only you believe in yourself. You should never settle for less than the best, no matter what you do in life. Educate yourself and get as much knowledge as you can. This is why Esther was trained to be a queen. She needed to first acquire the knowledge of how a queen should walk, speak, and act with diplomacy. She had to acquire the education and not just depend on her looks.

Many of us can learn from Esther. It is not what's on the outside—our looks, our clothes, our possessions—that matter; rather it is what we possess on the inside: our heart and our mind. Pursuing education and knowledge is a worthy goal, but the knowledge of God should be your primary pursuit. Knowledge is a key that unlocks opportunities in life. God provides the doors of opportunity; knowledge provides the key. This is why God tells us to study His word, life's instruction manual. How else can we learn about God and His kingdom? When we seek God, our purpose is in continued pursuit of us. God reveals it to us when we seek Him. It is our responsibility to acquire knowledge and understanding so that we can be equipped to receive our purpose in due time.

As parents or siblings, we need to be mindful of the royalty that is living within our home. In order to understand how God our Father views us as His children, many of us have children of our own. Once you understand that a life depends on you, you have a renewed sense of purpose. It is your responsibility to provide a safe place for your children to learn and grow; God will establish their path. Often we think of the safe place as the home, but it is sometimes a state of mind. If you provide a safe state of mind for others to dream, be educated, and believe in themselves, you provide a place where they can grow and prosper. The story of Esther is a reminder to us that sometimes there are kings and queens living among us, and we are to groom them, and allow ourselves to be groomed, for that position of purpose. It is not only our parents that can train or teach us, but others that God put as influential figures in our life can lead us in the right way to go.

Humility will allow our purpose to be manifested. It is not by knowledge alone, but by humility and service as well. The meaningful things we do in life are born out of purpose and will impact the world and be echoed throughout eternity. We are reading about Esther fulfilling her purpose because what she did will echo for generations to come. An orphan girl can become queen of a vast empire and empower her people to survive and thrive. Esther had to be queen to be able to fulfill her purpose, and she was empowered and prepared to do so. She did what others may have thought to be impossible, but with God, nothing is impossible.

God's favor rested on Esther, but His instruction came to King Xerxes as he tried to sleep. The story illustrates that because Xerxes could not rest, he called for the book of the chronicles of his kingship to be read and discovered the good that Mordecai had done to save his life. Mordecai had exposed an assassination attempt years earlier, and the king wanted to reward Mordecai. His purpose and Esther's purpose were working together for the good of their people.

At every level be prepared for the challenges your purpose will bring, and be ready to perform to the best of your ability. The power of Esther's purpose grew as her position changed. She accepted her purpose, became queen, and was able to deliver her people and give them the provision to sustain their life. God gave Joseph the provisions for his purpose at every level, too. In every position that Joseph held, he performed to the best of his ability, whether in the jailhouse, court-house, or the king's house. Prepare yourself through education, dedication, hard work, and integrity, and God will provide the opportunity and provision so you are prepared when your purpose, along with His many blessings, overtakes you.

Your purpose will always provide the provisions for its manifestation. That provision may be power, persuasion, promotion, position, or patience. Esther's purpose took her from the position of orphan girl to queen. She was patient as she waited for God to remove Queen Vashti and promote her to queen. She was persuasive in the presence of the king. She received the promotion to use her power, position, and persuasion to King Xerxes on behalf of her people.

Similarly, Moses was moved from an abandoned boy to a prince in Pharaoh's palace. Although he became a prince, he always knew his position with his people. His physical position did not dictate his disposition toward his own people. Moses' purpose was to free his people, and he needed to understand the mind of Pharaoh and the life of royalty to be able to relate to him. God had him raised as a prince, but Moses could not deliver his people in that position. He became an exile from Pharaoh's kingdom and gained power not from his position, but from his disposition. Moses was more powerful as an exile than when he was the prince of Egypt, because as an exile God revealed His purpose to him. God gave Moses the power to perform signs and wonders to demonstrate to Pharaoh that He and He alone was God. Moses' purpose was so potent that the most powerful man in the land, Pharaoh, could not stand against it. The deliverance came by the mighty hand of God through the humble hands of Moses.

There are times in this life when demands and responsibilities are greater than resources. These are the times when God demonstrates that He is the provider and will give the provisions for the purpose. Have you ever been in a situation where you felt overwhelmed and resources were not available? Have you wondered how you were going to make it when all your strength, resources, health, and abilities were exhausted? You are not alone. We all experience the anxiety of not having enough of something to make a difference. It's not always financial; it can be a depletion of physical, mental, emotional, or spiritual strength. I have been in situations where I did not have enough money to pay the bills or meet my obligations. My children wanted or needed something, and I did not have enough money to provide for my family the way I wanted to. In other situations, I have felt that I was not qualified to perform a particular job or make a difference. But when I refocus my faith away from my inadequacies and inabilities and focus on my Creator's ability, I realize that I have more power than I thought. There are many ways to solve problems, and I am equipped with the tools to perform the task. Sometimes the greatest obstacles we ever face are the ones we imagine but never experience. In other words, fear can cause us to focus on non-issues and make them bigger than they really are. When you focus on the manifestation of your purpose, you will often find that you have already been trained with the abilities to function within that purpose. I can rise above my circumstances, not by myself, but with the help of my Creator.

When operating in the purpose of God, God provides for the purpose. God may produce supernatural blessings to fulfill a purpose. It may be a case where God provides a vision to warn and foretell of some future disaster. He revealed the fate of Egypt to Joseph and advised him to store up an abundance so that the land would have food during the time of lack. God may reposition you in order for you to receive the provisions for the purpose. Esther was an orphan but was purposed by God to deliver her people. God repositioned Esther to be queen, and she had all the resources of King Xerxes at her disposal. He repositioned Joseph as governor of the foreign land of Egypt.

Even Jesus's disciples experienced a time when the demands were greater than the resources. The Bible tells of the story where Jesus called on His disciples to find food for 5,000 people. They informed him that there was no way they could feed the people because there were only five loaves of bread and two fish. What they failed to realize was that they could not provide food for the multitude, but God could. "With man this is impossible, but with God all things are possible."[32] The disciples made the mistake of focusing on their inabilities instead of God's abilities.

We err when we try to find our purpose on our own and then naturally try to find the provisions for the purpose that we think we've discovered. Whenever we rationalize a situation, we use our finite minds, but whenever we spiritualize the situation, we use the infinite mind of God. The lesson God demonstrates is that He will never leave us without provision. In fact, in this example, after the multitude ate, there was some left over. The Bible says, "And my God shall supply all your need according to His riches in glory by Christ Jesus."[33] You need not doubt that God will supply the provision for the purpose because He will not withhold any good thing from you. This is the reason Christ came to fulfill the ultimate purpose of God: to redeem mankind and offer salvation and freedom from sin and bondage.

When you seek God and keep His commandments, He reveals His purpose for your life and withholds "no good thing from you." He gives the provision needed to fulfill your purpose. "For the Lord God is a sun and shield; the Lord bestows favor and honor; no good thing does he withhold from those whose walk is blameless."[34]

Chapter Three
A Longing Fulfilled

৩৩

"Hope deferred makes the heart sick, but a longing fulfilled is a tree of life."

PROVERBS 13:12 NIV

"True happiness is not attained through self-gratification, but through fidelity to a worthy purpose."

HELEN KELLER

"There is a longing in all of us to fill the holes in our lives, holes in our finances and family, holes made by our failures. These holes can only be filled by the Holy One who can take our holes and make us whole."

RICARDO A. RICHARDSON

Have you ever desired to do something meaningful? Or felt you knew in your heart of hearts that you were created to be someone special? Many of us have heard some variations of these questions: "What will you do with your life?" "Why don't you make something of your life?" God put a longing within each of us to fulfill our purpose through serving Him. King Solomon knew this when he wrote, "A longing fulfilled is sweet to the soul."[35] Some people look to fill this void with fame, money, power, or position. Others look to fill it with relationships and love. The Creator is the only one who can fulfill the longing He placed within His creation. He is the one who can bring that perfect person into your life because the longing they have is filled by you and vice versa. My wife, Candice, is that perfect person God created especially for me. Or perhaps your longing is to know what you are designed for and what you are supposed to do in life. That fulfillment can come only from the Creator.

We often hear about what we need to do with our lives, because life is a gift for us to do something with. Whenever we give a gift, it is for an intended use, usually to the benefit of the receiver and the ultimate delight of the giver. God gave us the gift of life, and He delights in this gift when we do something with it.

Just as life is a gift, so is purpose. The purpose for life is contained within life itself. In order to really "do" something with our lives, we need to be influenced by our purpose and understand its power and potency. Your gift is always to help others and will ultimately fulfill the purpose that lies within you. Everything that was designed was designed not for itself, but to fulfill a purpose. The computer and Internet were designed for specific reasons, and they are perfected when working together. You and I were designed the same way, not for ourselves, but to help others. This dispels the notion that a man is an island unto himself. There should be nothing selfish about your existence. You were created for a reason that will make a difference in the lives of others to the glory of God and to the benefit of yourself. Our life is a gift to be given or, in other words, our purpose is a gift to be given to others to help them understand their purpose, which will, in turn, be given to others. Our purpose in life always gives us access to positions and places we would not otherwise experience. Purpose is a gift from God, and it will take you where you would not otherwise go. When you operate in it, you will find yourself in the presence of royalty.

King Solomon stated, "A man's gift makes room for him, and brings him before great men."[36] I experienced this when I visited India, Ethiopia, Tanzania, and the Kingdom of Swaziland in Africa. I was still young and searching for my purpose, but ended up meeting with presidents and kings at their palaces to discuss the lack of clean drinking water issues facing their respective countries. I joined Water For Life Foundation as vice chairman and helped shape the organization's vision, which was to deliver clean, safe, uncontaminated drinking water to the continent of Africa and globally. The foundation proposed to use technology that could instantly clean virus- and bacteria-infested water. This was the sole reason for my meeting with President Girma Wolde-Giorgis of Ethiopia, President Jakaya Kikwete of Tanzania, King Mswati III of Swaziland, and the high ministers in India. Here I am, a young man from the Bahamas, meeting with kings, presidents, and high ministers throughout the world! It was not my education, position, or money that created this opportunity. It was a purpose manifested by God.

I recall visiting the private palace bedroom of Emperor Haile Selassie of Ethiopia. We were guests of the president's son, so we had a private tour of the residence. My purpose was making room for me, bringing me into the presence of great men. It was a purpose that was greater than I. Our goal was to take the Water For Life Foundation to the world to address the lack of clean water, which had spawned an epidemic of enteric diseases. The foundation continued to fuel a longing I had to make a difference in the lives of people globally and began to shape my thinking about using purpose to affect change in the lives of others for the better. This is a common theme of purpose.

The Solomon Project Foundation was another foundation I developed with my wife, Candice, and a childhood friend, Derek. The title *Solomon Project* purposefully aligns this foundation with the task God gave King Solomon of building His house. God gave David the vision, but the task was given to Solomon. Through this foundation, we plan to build leadership centers to house and instruct men and women to live victoriously through wisdom, knowledge, and purpose given from their Creator. The centers will be based on the Christian faith, focusing on teaching about purpose, leadership, and service to others. I discussed this vision with pastor and mentor Dr. Myles Munroe, who was given a similar vision and purpose to create leadership centers around the world to equip and empower men and women to live the life God intended for them as kingdom citizens. Dr. Munroe instructs men and women to become leaders through the International Third World Leadership Association and Bahamas Faith Ministries International, domiciled in the Bahamas Islands. This is a purpose that I am longing to fulfill as God directs, and I hope to work with other men of God like Dr. Munroe to fulfill this awesome ministry.

In spite of envy and jealousy that others display toward you because of your purpose, your gifted purpose will make room for you. In fact, your gift was designed to feed off the jealousy and envy of others. God will increase the power of your purpose to show those around you that nothing can prevail against you. The harder people try to bring you down, the more potent your purpose becomes. In today's society, the word *haters* is a popular term used for those who display jealously, malice, and discord. But God can use our haters to bless us. Your haters are just as important as your friends. Your haters are the ones who expose you and bring out your true character. Judas exposed Jesus for who He was and is: He is the Savior in the face of those who love or hate Him, those who accept or reject Him. Judas was necessary, just as your haters are necessary.

Friends and family may stop your success if they try to protect you from challenges and failures in life. Those very failures and valleys are what shape your character and define your life. But loved ones don't want to see you struggle, be opposed, or persecuted; they want to protect you. This is how they show their love and concern. On the other hand, haters apply challenges and difficulties in your life in order for you to fail, but God uses them for your benefit and His glory. Just as a weight lifter develops strength by tearing down the muscle, we develop our spiritual muscles by the weight others put on us in the way of problems, burdens, and other life issues. Your haters unknowingly train your spiritual muscles and act as a catalyst to fulfill your purpose. Elijah had Jezebel, Moses had Pharaoh, Joseph had his brothers, David had Saul, and Jesus had Judas, scribes, and Pharisees. The Almighty God has the ultimate hater and adversary, Satan.

Opposition can come not only from people, but from conditions as well. Nelson Mandela had apartheid, and Martin Luther King had racial and social injustice. These conditions created a climate that exposed these respective leaders to fulfill their true purpose, to cause change for the better. Peter told Jesus that he would not be crucified and die; but Jesus spoke to the spirit of Peter, stating that he was being used by Satan to oppose that which God purposed, the death of the Christ. God uses what people do to us in hate into what He can use for our good. Your hater will be your mode of transportation to your destiny and to your purpose. He or she will unknowingly carry you to your place of destiny. Joseph's brothers carried him and were used by God to promote him to his promise and dream. Your friends and family may not promote progress through struggle, but your haters help promote progress, because God uses them as the necessary means to get you to your destiny and operate in your purpose! Our haters propel us to our destiny. God said that they are necessary because He will prepare a table in the presence of our enemies (haters).[37] So the more haters in your life, the bigger your feast will be. Joseph had many haters, and look what God prepared for him! Joseph stored all the grain in the land and when there was a seven-year famine, he had an abundance of food! God indeed prepared a veritable feast for Joseph, and all the people, including his brothers, bore witness.

Haters have been a welcomed part of my life dating back to high school. In college, I experienced hate in the form of racism. As a Bahamian, I had never personally experienced racism because blacks are a majority in the Bahamas. We had black leaders in politics, law enforcement, business, clergy, and every social and economic position of influence. In school, we didn't see color. Many of my teachers and friends were white. We were all Bahamians, all one nationality. So the hate growing up in the Bahamas was not racially motivated, but socially and economically based. Throughout my adult life, there were haters envious of my position and my purpose. I came to realize that those people were not focused on what purpose God had intended for them and became a tool that God used in order to promote and progress me and others whose purpose was revealed to them. Jesus assures us that people will hate us because of our purpose, but remember, they hated him first, and he possessed the ultimate purpose—salvation and redemption of mankind.

When I think of perseverance through difficult circumstances and ridicule from haters, I think of the life of Arthur Ashe, who became one of the most influential professional tennis players in history. He understood that success was about the obstacles that he had to overcome. Booker T. Washington once said, "I have learned that success is to be measured not so much by position that one has reached in life as by the obstacles which he has to overcome while trying to succeed."[38] He could have substituted *haters* in place of *obstacles* and the quote would still have the same meaning.

Arthur Ashe is an example of a purposeful life, allowing his gift to make room for him and ushering him into places most did not venture. The more others tried to stop him from succeeding, the further he went in his career. Ashe was the first African-American male to win a Grand Slam tennis event. In fact, he remains the only African-American player ever to win the men's singles tennis matches at Wimbledon, the US Open, or Australian Open. Additionally, he is one of only two black men, including France's Yannick Noah, to win a Grand Slam singles title. With all the professional tennis accomplishments and accolades he received, he was best known for his support of civil rights and AIDS causes globally. Ashe used his position of influence to change the position of people of African ancestry around the world.

Ashe was born in the segregated South during a time of racial inequality and injustice. He was a crusader for racial equality because of his racial experiences both growing up and during his tennis career. God used his childhood experiences to shape the way he would approach life and how he would help and serve others. He was looking at life through the right lenses and saw a vision of how America could be without racial injustice. He used his platform as a world-renowned professional to fight the causes that meant the most to him. He inspired millions because of his tennis profession and millions more because of his stance on racial injustice and equality. He also touched the lives of millions of people with AIDS. Some would say that Ashe's purpose was to be the first African-American to win the US Open tennis championship, but that was just a part of what shaped his purpose in life. Ashe was once quoted as saying, "I believe that I was destined to do more than just hit tennis balls."[39] And reflecting on his life's accomplishments and hardships, he said, "If I were to say, God, why me, about the bad things, then I should have said God, why me, about the good things that happened in my life."[40]

The world we live in is increasingly self-indulgent and self-centered. People focus on financial independence, social acceptance, and recognition. Celebrities' lives are coveted because they are positioned in society as having it all: a glamorous life, money, prestige, recognition, position, and fame. They are increasingly known by one name, when others are only recognized by their family name or, more commonly, their celebrity name. This is the culture in which we live. No wonder we are wrapped up in the idea that we have to find our purpose through success and wealth; it is a self-centered, self-seeking endeavor. All these possessions do not bring joy or happiness to one's life. There is still a longing in us that needs fulfilling. For many of us, we walk around with holes in our lives—holes from past hurts, hang-ups, and disappointments. We have holes in our families, holes in our finances, the hole of no purpose, and holes in our spirituality, which limit our functioning correctly or cause us to malfunction. We act like everything is fine when we long for the hole of purpose to be filled.

God is full of holiness. Yes, He is perfect and holy in every way, but I like to think that His holiness comes from the fact that he can fill all of our holes. Jesus says, "Come to Me, all you who labor and are heavy-laden *and* overburdened and I will cause you to rest [I will ease and relieve and refresh your souls]. Take My yoke upon you and learn of Me, for I am gentle (meek) and humble (lowly) in heart, and you will find rest (relief and ease and refreshment and recreation and blessed quiet) for your souls. For My yoke is wholesome (useful, good—not harsh, hard, sharp, or pressing, but comfortable, gracious, and pleasant), and My burden is light *and* easy to be borne."[41] God wants you to cast your cares, your issues, your quest for purpose, and your worries upon Him. He is the only one who can take all of your holes and make you whole.

Once we understand that the divine purpose of God is the only purpose of God, and it is the only one we need for our lives, we will begin to find contentment. God, in His infinite wisdom, will manifest a singular purpose that is a larger part of His divine purpose for humanity and His kingdom. We have to put aside our own personal self-interest and take on the issues of people and the kingdom of God. Whenever Jesus performed a healing or gave a blessing, it was always intended for the multitude, not just the individual, although the individual received a personal blessing from it.

God told Jeremiah that he was born for a purpose, as we all are. God said, "Before I formed you in the womb I knew you, before you were born I set you apart; I appointed you as a prophet to the nations."[42] God's purpose for Jeremiah was as a prophet, sanctified and ordained as God's voice to the nations. Jeremiah was unwilling to accept the responsibility and purpose God revealed to him. Even then, he told God that he did not know how to speak because he was only a child and was too young to be a prophet. "But the Lord said to me, 'Do not say, "I am too young." You must go to everyone I send you to and say whatever I command you. Do not be afraid of them, for I am with you and will rescue you,' declares the Lord."[43] Then the Lord touched the mouth of Jeremiah and declared that he had put the words in his mouth. Today, God has appointed (manifested his purpose) Jeremiah over nations and kingdoms to uproot and tear down, to destroy and overthrow, to build and to plant.[44] Jeremiah knew that he would not be popular if he proclaimed the word of God as directed. Many preachers today have the same fear and stay away from the things God says for fear of not being popular with the congregation. Jeremiah knew he would not be liked among the nations, but often God's purpose for our lives is not for popularity, although He will make your name known throughout the earth by His divine purpose for your life. Like Jeremiah, you were born of purpose, and God wants to reveal it to you.

As a young executive officer for RealMed Corporation, a healthcare technology company based in Indiana, I had the opportunity to visit Washington, DC with my business associates to lobby the Medical Savings Accounts (MSAs), healthcare administration accounts promoted by J. Patrick Rooney. Pat Rooney, my business mentor and friend, was a very wealthy insurance executive, chairman of Golden Rule Insurance Company, now United Healthcare, and a man of principle. Pat recruited me to work as an actuary for Golden Rule when I graduated from St. John's University, our alma mater. He was a humble man who had a heart for children. Golden Rule Insurance Company was lobbying for the passage of legislation that allowed use of MSAs in large corporations while RealMed was lobbying because we had developed the administration software for the MSA accounts.

Upon one of our visits to DC, I met our driver, a chauffeur named Albert Fox. Al was assigned to drive us to the various meetings with senators and representatives on Capitol Hill. One evening I asked Al to pick me up and show me the city, and he accepted. I remember how surprised he was to see me with the group and told me that he was happy to see a young black executive in that capacity. I told him that God had opened doors for me that I could not, and I shared my faith, as my position was meant for a purpose. We then began to share about our goals and plans. He told me about his, Community Youth Connection Inc. (CYC), a 501c3 non-profit organization. To his surprise, I was excited to learn about it, and I told him that I wanted to not only contribute to it but to become personally involved. I recognized Al was serving the underprivileged school children from area schools, and this was indeed a worthy purpose and cause. His organization chose the neediest children from area schools and purchased clothing, school supplies, and groceries for their families. Al had such a passion for the children. Al had a desire and longing to see the children given an opportunity to learn without worrying about basic necessities such as clothing and meals. His longing, not for his purpose but for the provision of having it realized, was fulfilled when the *Washington Post* ran a story on him, and Oprah Winfrey invited him to appear on her show, *Spirit of Giving*. On the show, Al received an $80,000 donation from Sears to shop for the children and other gifts from Oprah and her corporate sponsors. Al continues to fulfill his purpose today and has extended his program to serve underprivileged children in schools around the country. CYC continues its program and has seen a dramatic improvement in the grades and lives of the children it supports.

I am still a close friend of Al, and I am an active board member of the CYC foundation. Although Al worked as a chauffeur, he was called by God for a purpose, a longing that was fulfilled. It doesn't matter what work you do, you can still allow your purpose to be fulfilled as long as you do it unto the Lord and not to people. Many people are actually doing what they were meant to do but without purpose. They are working, but not as unto the Lord. In other words, they are working for a paycheck, promotion, or their own selfish desires. Don't get me wrong, wanting a better job that pays more is good, but you cannot focus only on that aspect because you will miss the most important reason. Operating in whatever you do in the spirit of serving will give you more fulfillment than just money, because there is always a higher-paying job out there. If that is your only focus, you will be chasing but never finding fulfillment. Further, your purpose is not for the position; rather your position is for your purpose. Al used his position as a driver to connect with many powerful businessmen and politicians in Washington to promote CYC for underprivileged children throughout the United States. Al is operating in the purpose God intended for him and now recognizes that he was created to make a difference in the lives of the youths in his community. Al understands what King David, the psalmist, knew about his purpose: It was created and formed before he was born. He says,

For you created my inmost being; you knit me together in my mother's womb. I praise you because I am fearfully and wonderfully made; your works are wonderful, I know them full well. My frame was not hidden from you when I was made in the secret place. When I was woven together in the depths of the earth, your eyes saw my unformed body. All the days ordained for me were written in your book before one of them came to be.[45]

It could not be plainer that God is the one who creates and forms us. Yes, your father and mother were chosen to bring you into the world through natural causes, but it is God that formed you, formed purpose within you. When I came into the world, my mother, as all mothers do, was waiting for my cry to ensure that I would live. She felt that I was a special child, as all mothers feel about their newly-born babies. You are special because God made you Himself. God made you for a purpose. What our mothers feel is exactly what God desires. It does not matter if your parents acknowledge it, you are a special person born for a special purpose. My purpose here is to tell you that you are one of God's miracles. You are already special because you were born. Do you know that God designed you a winner?

According to the World Health Organization, a healthy adult male can release an average of 100 million sperm in a single ejaculation. Lauralee Sherwood documents that an average human ejaculate contains about 180 million sperm (66 million/mL), but some ejaculates can contain as many as 400 million sperm![46] Sperm motility, which is the ability for the sperm to work its way to the egg, can range from five to sixty-eight minutes.[47] By contrast, women are born with an average of 1-2 million egg follicles, the functional anatomical structure that produces female gamete (eggs). By puberty, most of those follicles close up, and only about four hundred to four hundred fifty will ever release mature eggs for fertilization. But if it only takes the union of one sperm and one egg to create a baby, why do men produce such a whopping number of sperm? Wouldn't it be less wasteful for a man to release one or two to meet one egg?

The reason for this curiosity can be answered in two words: *sperm competition*. The sperm motility of hundreds of million of sperm competing for a limited number of eggs demonstrates the competitive nature that exists in all of us. We want to win, but in fact we have won already! God purposed it that you would be born a winner. He made our purpose so potent that we were victorious against billions of other sperm. In fact, victory is the fulfillment of purpose realized. So if your Creator created you a winner, how can you live a defeated life? You had a purpose to be born, and that is why you won! You outswam more than 1.2 billion sperm to make sure you fulfilled your initial purpose, which was conception and birth so that you could operate in your life's purpose. So stay connected to the Creator who made you a winner and let Him guide your life, manifest your purpose for living, and help you live a victorious and purposeful life. You were born a champion! You were born a winner! You were born with purpose! You were formed by the Creator, and He coached you to have victory.[48] Greater is the purpose in you than any plans in the world! You can overcome anything, just as you overcame the billion other competitors for the prize, the gift that is your life. The fact is that your purpose drove you to win and overcome.

Jesus' purpose drove Him to win, and our belief in Him will help us overcome. The writer of 1 John wrote, "Who is it that overcomes the world?" The New Living Translation states, "And who can win this battle against the world? Only those who believe that Jesus is the Son of God."[49] So, as your purpose drove you to overcome and win the gift of your natural, physical life, Jesus' purpose for salvation allowed you to overcome the world for you to win the gift of the spiritual, eternal life.

As we review the gift of purpose of individuals of our time, we uncover that just as Jesus' main purpose was salvation, so will ours be. How? I'm glad you asked. The Bible records that "Those who say they live in God should live their lives as Jesus did."[50] And Jesus' life and purpose was to serve mankind and set us free, for whoever the Son sets free is indeed free. Again Jesus said, "Just as the

Son of Man did not come to be served but to serve, and to give His life a ransom for many."[51] So, God wants us to be modeled after His son. If we are to live at the core, we will ultimately live a life that is serving others through our purpose. Think of it this way: Someone who dedicates their life to teaching children is ultimately doing what? Setting them free from illiteracy. What about the policeman, fireman, doctor, cook, social worker, dietician, counselor, or even janitor? They provide a service that frees us from crime, injury, illness, hunger, etc. This is why Paul says in his letter to the Colossians, "Work willingly at whatever you do, as though you were working for the Lord rather than people."[52] When we operate at the core, we understand that our assignment is from God, and we work as though we work unto our Creator, not people. Then we will live a fulfilling life in the service of humanity, making a difference in ours and in others' lives.

Chapter Four
Identity of Purpose

☙❧

"For the Lord sees not as man sees: man looks on the outward appearance, but the Lord looks on the heart."

1 SAMUEL 16:7

"The ultimate measure of a man is not where he stands in moments of comfort, but where he stands at times of challenge and controversy."

DR. MARTIN LUTHER KING JR.

"Be more concerned with your character than your reputation, because your character is what you really are, while your reputation is merely what others think you are.

COACH JOHN WOODEN

"Your reputation is what others think about you, but your identity is what God knows about you, so instead of trying to build your reputation, focus on confirming your identity."

RICARDO A. RICHARDSON

You are more than who people say you are. You are more than your title, your job, and your relationships. These things do not define you, so they cannot confine you. Only your Creator can name you or blame you. Others who try to name you ultimately try to blame you. They govern your life based on the reputation that was created for you. Your identity does not lie in whom you are with, who you are married to, or even who you are related to. It lays in what God names you and how He sees you. Your name is the most important descriptive that you have, but unless you are named by the Creator, you have no identity.

In Biblical times, a name meant everything. Leah named her sons based on her own disposition. God blessed her with children, but she took out her frustrations through her children's names. Her firstborn son she named Rueben. The first part of his name in Hebrew is "Ra'ah" and the second part is "ye-ehaboni," which translated is "the Lord has seen my affliction or pain," and "my husband will love me" (Gen. 29:32). Her second son she named Simeon because "the Lord heard [Shama] that I was unloved" (Gen. 29:33). Leah was most concerned about what people would say about her and what they called her. She was not the first choice of wife by Jacob, who loved her younger sister, Rachel, more than her. But God blessed Leah with children, while Rachel was barren, yet Leah did not focus on the blessing but on her reputation. She missed her identity. Once you realize that your reputation is not your identity, you will be able to seek the Giver of both identity and purpose.

Do you know who one of the most feared and ruthless Jewish rebels in Jesus' day was? He was a notorious criminal. The Bible says that he was bound with chains with others that made insurrection with him. In other words, all those in rebellion against the Romans had been led by this man. He was essentially an enemy of the state and of the Roman Empire. His name was Barabbas. His reputation was deserved. Barabbas had committed crimes against the Romans that would result in his death by crucifixion. He was on death row, and Pilate, the Roman governor in Jesus' time on earth, held his fate in his hands. The Romans feared and hated Barabbas. Barabbas knew that because of his crimes against Rome, his only release from a life of prison, bondage, and chains would be his death on a cross. The Bible gives the account in Mark of the choice given to the people to release Barabbas or Jesus:

> Now it was the custom at the festival to release a prisoner whom the people requested. A man called Barabbas was in prison with the insurrectionists who had committed murder in the uprising. The crowd came up and asked Pilate to do for them what he usually did.
>
> "Do you want me to release to you the king of the Jews?" asked Pilate, knowing it was out of self-interest that the chief priests had handed Jesus over to him. But the chief priests stirred up the crowd to have Pilate release Barabbas instead.
>
> "What shall I do, then, with the one you call the king of the Jews?" Pilate asked them
>
> "Crucify him!" they shouted.
>
> "Why? What crime has he committed?" asked Pilate.
>
> But they shouted all the louder, "Crucify him!"

Wanting to satisfy the crowd, Pilate released Barabbas to them. He had Jesus flogged and handed him over to be cruicitied.[53]

It is interesting that we never hear about Barabbas terrifying the people after his release from death row. He may have gone back to his life of crime or may have realized that Jesus saved his life, literally. The innocent Jesus took the guilty Barabbas' place. Can you imagine what Barabbas was thinking when this occurred? He'd probably heard about Jesus while he was leading rebellions against the Romans. Now, here he stands in the presence of Pilate, the Roman, and Jesus, the Jew. Pilate wanted to crucify Barabbas because of the sins he had committed, while God wanted to save Barabbas from his sins.

The Bible does not reference Barabbas as the son of a father as it does with other men. I believe that Barabbas found his true identity the day Jesus died for his sins. The prefix "Bar" means "son of," and "Abba" means father. On the cross, Jesus cried out "Abba," which means father. Barabbas was saved that day, and because Jesus called God "Abba," He gave Barabbas an identity as a son of God the Father, as He did for you and me. Barabbas now knew his true identity because of what Jesus called him, not who men said he was. Barabbas was always a son of the Creator, as we all are; he just didn't know his identity.

Jesus asked of his disciples, "Who do men say I am?" He was talking specifically about his reputation; but as he explained, his reputation was not the identity of his purpose. He wanted to know if his disciples or men knew his true identity or just his reputation. This question is one that many of us have contemplated ourselves: Who do people say that we are or what do they think of us? For those of you still searching for the meaning of your existence in your seasoned years, it is not unusual to be in this place of deep introspection about your life. For others, there is still this sense of wanting to know who you are and wanting to be accepted by others. How many times have you said, "I want to accomplish this or that by the time I'm a certain age"? Oftentimes, when we are unable to achieve our goals by our self-appointed deadlines, we become discouraged and frustrated. For those who have not yet discovered their purpose and identity, recognize that you need to turn to God. In desperation say, "Lord, I desire to do Your will and accomplish all that You would have me do, because what is for me is for me, amen."

Often, our motives for crying out to God are backward: We want the blessing, so we decide to do His will. But we need to desire to do His will as our primary motivation (put Him first) and be pleased when His blessings follow. Jesus teaches us a valuable lesson about our identity of purpose:

When Jesus came to the region of Caesarea Philippi, he asked his disciples, "Who do people say that the Son of Man is?" They replied, "Some say John the Baptist; others say Elijah; and still others, Jeremiah or one of the prophets." "But what about you?" He asked. "Who do you say I am?" Simon Peter answered, "You are the Christ, the Son of the living God." Jesus replied, "Blessed are you, Simon son of Jonah, for this was not revealed to you by man, but by my Father in heaven."[54]

In fact, when Jesus was baptized by John the Baptist, God affirmed His identity by stating with a loud voice from heaven, "This is my beloved son, in whom I am well pleased."[55] God honored Jesus by affirming who He is, as Peter did when he called Jesus the Christ.

We see from the conversation with the disciples that even Jesus demonstrates that it is okay to ponder the question about what people think of you. But the important thing is, He demonstrates that your reputation may or may not reflect your identity of purpose. The people were saying that He was someone else, drawing from past characters with whom they could identify. They were trying to label Jesus, similar to what people do to each other. But Peter did not draw from a past character but from one who is past, present, and future, the Christ, Son of the living God. Jesus revealed himself as both man and God, depending on what people saw and believed. But regardless of what men believed, He always is the beloved Son of God and the savior. The first answers the disciples gave were based on the physical being of Jesus, on what people believed, that he was just like Elijah, John, or some other man who preceded him. But Peter gave an answer based on his spiritual sense of Jesus, which was given to him by the Creator. Jesus then tells Peter that his answer was revealed to him from God the Father. Jesus blessed Peter for the words he spoke and the answer he gave, because Peter was influenced by the Spirit of God.

I love the game of basketball and had aspirations of playing professionally. Many of my peers and fans thought I was good enough to play in the NBA. My reputation as a basketball player grew throughout the Bahamas. I tried identifying with this reputation, but playing basketball was not the only thing I did well. I had other passions I wanted to pursue but only displayed what others wanted me to: basketball. I was fortunate to be able to play in college and then later become the CEO of the Continental Basketball Association, the league that developed NBA players and coaches like Phil Jackson, the former Chicago Bulls and Los Angeles Lakers coach, George Karl, head coach of the Denver Nuggets, and Rick Carlisle, head coach of the Dallas Mavericks. I met a number of professional players and coaches who were men of purpose outside of professional sports.

One man in particular, Coach John Wooden, was one of the most successful basketball coaches in US history. He began his coaching career in 1932 as a high school coach in Kentucky. He won ten NCAA titles, seven in a row with the UCLA Bruins. He was named the Coach of the Century in 1999 by ESPN. He received the Presidential Medal of Freedom in 2003, the highest civilian honor America can give. He was an author, speaker, and life coach. The Legends of Hardwood, which held its inaugural event in 1997, is a marquee celebration during the Men's Final Four basketball weekend. The event honors character, integrity, and faith in sports and features the presentation of the Coach Wooden "Keys to Life" Award. I was fortunate to spend some one-on-one time with Coach Wooden at the Legends of the Hardwood event at the 2000 NCAA Final Four Championship in Indianapolis, Indiana. I served on the Legends board that year along with Athletes in Action and the Fellowship of Christian Athletes. Coach Wooden shared his Keys to Life with me, as he often did with others. We spoke about my basketball career and journey. He asked me details about my career. I told him I averaged more than thirty points per game throughout high school and was considered one of the best young players when I played. He smiled and then said, "Ricardo, I wish I could have recruited (from) Nassau (Bahamas)!"

He had a way of brightening everyone's day with kind words and a contagious smile. So much of his legacy is focused on the basketball dynasty that he built, incorporating teamwork and organization. But Coach Wooden lived out his faith and beliefs. He boycotted the 1946 NAIA tournament while coaching at Indiana State because Clarence Walker, the one black player on his team, was not allowed to play. Of all his accomplishments, it was Coach Wooden's faith he cherished most. He was devoted to God, faith, and his wife, Nell. He realized that his purpose was bigger than coaching basketball; it was about coaching life. Looking at Coach Wooden's life, it is easy to see that he was a man of purpose. And anyone that had the opportunity to speak personally with him would come away understanding just why he was purpose driven. Whenever I have the opportunity to speak to young people about sports and life, I highlight the keys that Coach Wooden lived by. His Keys to Life:

1. Be true to yourself.
2. Help others.
3. Make each day your masterpiece.
4. Drink deeply from good books, especially the Bible.
5. Make friendship a fine art.
6. Build a shelter against a rainy day by the life you live.
7. Pray for guidance and counsel, and give thanks for your blessings each day.[56]

When you apply these keys to locked doors of opportunity, you are able to open them, walk through, and experience something new and different. Coach Wooden's keys will help you open locked doors in your life as purpose is revealed.

We have been discussing that your unique purpose will be revealed to you as you go deeper in God, the Creator of all purposes, ultimate, universal, and unique. The ultimate purpose of God was to create man in His likeness and image, and the universal purpose was to reveal His likeness to mankind. The unique purpose was for mankind to know Him through Jesus Christ. God revealed Jesus' purpose to Peter. He told Peter that Jesus is the Son of the living God; He is the universal Christ, savior of all men. Jesus embodied all three—ultimate, universal, and unique. Not only did God reveal His own purpose through Jesus, He also revealed Peter's purpose to him as well, and Peter didn't even ask for it. He told Peter that the Holy Spirit caused him to confess the true identity of the Christ, and this same Holy Spirit that revealed Jesus' identity is what Jesus would build the church upon. Jesus was the Rock of Ages, and Peter confessed this by the power given to him from the Father. The translation of Simon is "sand," and Peter is "little stone" in the Greek and Latin. Jesus knew that Peter would be weak and would later deny that he knew Him, but Peter demonstrated that the Creator could speak through him and influence his words, which was why he said that Jesus was the Christ. Peter allowed God to influence his thoughts so that he was able to confess the truth, but when Peter was influenced by his own thoughts and fear, he later denied he even knew the Christ. Even though Peter was easily influenced and was like "sand or small stone," when he allowed the power and the Spirit of the living God to influence his thoughts, he would be given the keys to heaven and act in the strength of Jesus, the Rock.[57]

Shortly after Jesus gave Peter this prophesy, He told him that He would fulfill His true purpose and redeem mankind. Peter rebuked Jesus when He told them that He would be killed by the elders, chief priest, and scribes. Jesus admonished Peter, saying, "Get behind me Satan!"[58] He tells Peter he is a hindrance because he is not setting his mind on the things of God but on the things of man. When Peter called Jesus the Son of the living God, he was setting his mind on the things of the Creator and was operating from the Spirit of God, which was why Jesus told him that he would possess the keys to heaven. But if he did not operate from the Spirit, Jesus called the adverse spirit that Peter demonstrated, only minutes after he praised him for the spirit, of Satan.

You and I are the same way in the eyes of the Creator and of the Christ. If we are influenced by Christ, we are solid like rocks and can do great things and fulfill our potential. But if we are not influenced by the mindset of Christ, we are like sand and small pebbles, ineffective in fulfilling our purpose and operating in the power of God. Peter made the decision to deny that he even knew Christ, but later when Peter preached the sermon at Pentecost, the Bible says that three thousand souls believed on the Christ and were saved.[59] He was under the influence of the Creator and able to fulfill his purpose and calling as he delivered this soul-stirring message.

One of the most important gifts that God has given man is the right to choose. We can even decide our own salvation. Joshua told the people, "This day I give you death and life, now you choose." Peter chose to deny Christ but later repented that decision. Decision is the only thing that gives man an identity, and a decision influenced by Christ identifies man as a child of God. It is your life, not anyone else's. Don't let other people make decisions about it. You can take counsel from them, but the final decision should be your own. Instead of choosing to have Christ renew their minds, many people cast their old mindset onto others. Your decision to choose to be influenced by the mindset of Christ—to decide to go deeper in God to receive the revelation of your purpose—is the most important decision you will make. And, by the way, deciding not to decide is also a decision.

Jesus, knowing how people saw Him, sometimes answered them according to their belief. A rich young ruler came to Jesus and addressed him as "good teacher."[60] Immediately Jesus asked him why he called him good. He went on to say that there is no one good but God. He knew that the young rich ruler saw himself as a good man and He was trying to equalize himself with Jesus. When Jesus told him to keep the commandments or the law, he stated that he had kept all of the law since he was a youth. Jesus knew that no one is perfect in the law; that is why God gives us grace. If our salvation were measured by the law, we would all fail. Jesus wanted the young man to know that the Creator of the law was God, and only He could be "perfectly good" in keeping the law.

Jesus also knew the difference between men worshiping Him as a man or as God. Often He would say, I and the Father are one, and in this occasion he told the young ruler, don't call me good, because there is none good but God. Men often wanted to worship a man, the creation, instead of worshiping God, the Creator. The young man may have elevated himself to that of the stature of Jesus because he felt that he was good. That is why he said good teacher, in order to establish that Jesus and he were good. Jesus corrected him by stating that God, holy and true, is good. Jesus talks about His spirituality and duality with God as well as His duality with man, but He teaches us to focus on the spiritual things of God, not the physical attributes of man. On another occasion, Pilate asked Jesus if He was the king of the Jews, and Jesus told him that it was just as he had asked. Jesus always knew His identity of purpose.

I often wondered why Jesus spoke in parables. Every prophet or man who spoke about the scriptures prior to Jesus spoke directly to the people to teach them about God. David wrote the psalms to God telling of His goodness and how to worship Him. Solomon wrote all the proverbs teaching plainly about knowledge, wisdom, and how to live. But then here comes Jesus, the Son of omniscient God, and He speaks in parables and riddles. In Matthew alone He shares the parables of the sower, hidden treasures, weeds, nets, mustard seeds, and yeast. He revealed to His disciples when they asked Him why he spoke in parables that the knowledge of the secrets of the kingdom of heaven had not been revealed to all men. He also says that though seeing, they do not see; though hearing, they do not hear or understand. In other words, His purpose and the purpose of men are not revealed unless God reveals it to them, just as God revealed Jesus's true identity to Peter.

Solomon, the wisest king that ever lived, understood that God conceals things and reveals them to the men that earnestly seek His revelation. He said, "It is the glory of God to conceal a thing: but the honour of kings is to search out a matter."[61] The prophet Isaiah proclaimed that Jesus would speak in parables when he said, "You will be ever hearing but never understanding; you will be ever seeing but never perceiving. For this people's heart has become callused; they hardly hear with their ears, and they have closed their eyes. Otherwise they might see with their eyes, hear with their ears, understand with their hearts and turn, and I would heal them."[62] So, we can see that God wants us to find the purpose for our existence, but we have to search Him to find it along with the glory of God to reveal it.

Jesus explains the parables and riddles to His disciples, and in each instance, He talks about the kingdom of God. He spoke in parables to hide the truth of the kingdom of God. Just as your purpose is hidden and is only revealed when you go deeper in Him, so are the true treasures of God's kingdom, which can be discovered only by seeking God. That is why Jesus told His disciples that the truths of the kingdom are revealed to them but not to everyone. Jesus spoke plainly to the people until the Pharisees and scribes denied His true identity. After their disbelief, Jesus spoke in parables so that those who truly desired to know Him would find Him. He knew that if a person wanted to understand a parable they would earnestly seek out the answer. The more they sought to understand, the more that would be revealed to them.

God's revelations are such that we need to have a ready, open, and willing mind to receive them. The task of searching, studying, and seeking God prepares our minds and hearts to receive those purposeful things of God that will fulfill us. The full knowledge of God is far beyond the grasp of man, but we can get a glimpse as to how the kingdom operates by applying our knowledge as to how creation operated. We understand that if a farmer sows seeds on a rocky path or among weeds, the crop will suffer. However, if he sows seed in fertile ground, while he may not understand how it grows and produces fruit, he trusts that it will. Creation is responsible for certain finite steps, like preparing the soil and planting the seed. But then the Creator takes over, doing what may seem impossible—sending rain, sunlight, and everything else necessary for the seed to produce a harvest. The farmer's purpose is similar to our purpose. We do finite things to prepare ourselves—acquiring education and knowledge—and the Creator does the seemingly impossible: granting opportunities we could not create ourselves.

God still speaks to His creation in parables and riddles, except now He uses the riddles of life. Each of us goes through life's mysteries searching to find our purpose. God designed it that way so we would seek and ask Him. The more we engage Him, the more He engages our purpose. There is a saying, "Take one step closer to God, and He will take two steps closer to you." In other words, search for God and He will reward your effort and fulfill what you are searching and longing for. To get closer to God, we must abide (remain) in His word and He will abide (remain) in us.[63] When we go a step further (no pun intended), God begins to reveal to us who we really are. When we lift God up through praise, meditating on His word, and abiding in Him, He draws us to himself. The Bible also quotes Jesus as saying, "And I, if I am lifted up from the earth, will draw all peoples to Myself."[64] We have the desire to find out our purpose, to search for the reason for living, to be drawn to our Creator, because God designed it that way, and when Jesus was lifted up on Cavalry's cross, He fulfilled that purpose.

I saw a sign in a small country church during the Christmas season that read Wise Men Still Seek Him. While this referenced the wise men that sought Christ at His birth, wise are the men of today who seek him for rebirth, for the meaning of life and existence.

God has an awesome purpose to reveal to you as well. The Bible says, "You do not have, because you do not ask God."[65] God invites us to ask Him for anything. We also know that God is a generous God and gives freely to anyone who asks Him and does not become irritated or angry that we ask Him.[66] In fact, He loves when we seek Him so that He can reveal all that He has for us, the truth about our lives, relationships, contentment, wisdom, love, and purpose. How many of you when asked by your son, daughter, father, mother, or friend would deny them? Each of us would give to our family and others in need when we are able. God is able to do exceedingly above everything that we can imagine, ask, or think. Jesus made reference to this when he said,

Ask and it will be given to you; seek and you will find; knock and the door will be opened to you. For everyone who asks receives; he who seeks finds; and to him who knocks, the door will be opened. Which of you, if his son asks for bread, will give him a stone? Or if he asks for a fish, will give him a snake?" If you, then, though you are evil, know how to give good gifts to your children, how much more will your Father in heaven give good gifts to those who ask him![67]

We all search for the reason for our existence, but we often ask the wrong people. If I wonder what others think of me, I am focusing on the created as opposed to the Creator. What others think is not as important as what I think of myself, and more importantly, what God knows of me. But when my purpose is revealed and I start living a life of purpose, then my reputation, or more specifically, my identity, will reflect that purpose. Others will begin to see the purpose of my life, and my purpose will answer the question of who I am.

Arthur Ashe talked about reputation and identity in his book *Days of Grace*.[68] He recognized his reputation as an image cultivated for the public and his identity as a reputation that is deserved. He stated,

> *If one's reputation is a possession, then of all of my possessions, my reputation means most to me. Nothing comes even close to it in importance. Now and then I have wondered whether my reputation means too much to me; but I can no more easily renounce my concern with what other people think of me more than I can will myself to stop breathing. No matter what I do, or where or when I do it, I feel the eyes of others on me, judging me. Needless to say, I know that a fine line exists between caring about one's reputation and hypocrisy. When I speak of the importance to me of my reputation, I am referring to a reputation that is deserved, not an image cultivated for the public in spite of the facts.*[69]

By following the commands that God gives you, it will shape your identity of purpose—a reputation deserved—and provide fertile ground for your purpose to be revealed and prevail. It is not as important for others to recognize who you are as it is for you to know who you are, and to recognize what God calls you. Your reputation is what others think about you, but your identity is what God knows about you.

An African emperor of Ethiopia sent a young speechwriter to an American university to study. I had the opportunity to sit with this man at his home when I visited Ethiopia in 2009. His name is Mengiste Desta, former ambassador and the author of *Ethiopia's Role in African History*.[70] He was sent to study in America to pursue a doctorate degree. At the university, he worked as a janitor, cleaning floors and taking care of the garbage. Everyone saw him as a lowly janitor, but he was used to manual labor in his country and saw it as a privilege to help provide a clean environment. He had servants in his country who did this work, but he was not beyond doing manual labor himself. He understood that before one could lead, one must be able to serve. When he returned to his native country, the emperor made him an ambassador. He always knew that he would return to assume a position of importance. He was a leader and was able to serve others. Mengiste did not let the opinion of others shape what he knew about himself. His identity of purpose was the same before and after he worked as a janitor.

The ultimate leader, Jesus, also knew that in order to lead, one must first be humble and be able to serve. Jesus would repeatedly state that He came to do the will of His Father. He made himself of "no reputation,"[71] according to the book of Philippians. He took on the role of a servant, although He was always King. He was not out to make a name for himself but rather to serve, understanding that in serving, God would elevate him and make His name above every name.[72] How often do we seek to make a name for ourselves with the thought that once we do, our purpose will be fulfilled? Through serving, we allow our Creator to elevate our name through the execution of our purpose. Jesus knew His purpose and therefore was able to serve His identity. He knew who He was. The Bible tells the story of Jesus washing the disciples' feet.[73] To paraphrase, at the last supper, Jesus sat with His twelve disciples and served them. He put a towel around his waist and kneeled to wash each of their feet. Peter protested saying, "I will not allow you to wash my feet, Teacher." Jesus said, "I am your teacher and leader, and if you do not let me wash your feet, you have no part in me. Also, if I can serve you, then in your position, you can serve others."

This is the most important trait of leaders. They must know how to serve and follow. Ambassador Desta was able to serve his fellow students by serving as a janitor. He was always a leader, even as a lowly janitor; he knew who he was in Christ. Jesus, too, knew his purpose, and nothing or no one would interfere with him fulfilling his purpose. Your purpose defines you. It identifies you with your Creator. You have to know who you are. Don't let others define you. Once you are adopted into the kingdom as a child of the King, you are called to live a kingdom life, full of purpose. Even if a prince or princess is moved to a peasant field, it does not change the fact that they are royalty. You are royalty in God's eyes because you are a part of His kingdom.

Who did Joseph's brothers say that he was? They called him a dreamer. Even his father scolded him when he told him about his dreams. Because of the contents of the dream, his brothers threw him in a pit and sold him as a slave to Egypt.

They tried to take his life and in so doing cancel out his purpose, which was to one day rule over them. The lesson here is that no one can define, confine, or cancel your purpose. It cannot be given to you nor taken away by any created being. People will try to define you so they can confine you, and so doing, elevate their own stature. Joseph's brothers and even his father, who loved him dearly, wanted to confine and define him and elevate themselves. But their plan, made in fear and anger, ended in the preservation of their very lives. Potiphar's wife, too, by her false accusations, tried to define him—as a rapist. But it is not as important who men say you are as it is about who God says you are. God called Joseph a visionary and a leader. Joseph knew who he was and whose he was, even when no one else did. He refused to let anyone influence his purpose in life.

People will often look to your title or position instead of your purpose, but you must stay focused on your purpose, not your position. In fact, people can only see your position; you are the only one that can see your purpose, so stay focused on it. God called Joseph a leader and gave him the assurance that he would rule. Despite the outward struggles Joseph faced, he always had God's favor. The Bible says that everywhere Joseph went, God was with him and blessed and prospered him. God gave him his high-ranking positions because of His purpose. I believe that you, too, can have God's favor in your life if you stay connected to Him. The purpose of life is not to get a better position; position is a result of purpose.

Who do people say you are? Do they think they are better than you? Do they say you are a follower, not a leader? Do they say you are a dreamer? Do they talk down to you or show jealousy? My friend, it is not important what they call you. What matters is who you believe you are and to what (and whom) you will answer. The Bible says, "Therefore, if any man be in Christ, he is a new creature; old things are passed away; behold, all things are become new."[74] We may have thought of ourselves differently because of what others thought, but God says once you understand your true identity in Christ, you become a new person with new thoughts. Stay focused on God because He is the one who calls you by your true name, your true identity. This is what God says about you: "The Lord will make you the head, and not the tail. If you pay attention to the commands of the Lord your God that I give you this day and carefully follow them, you will always be at the top, never at the bottom."[75]

God called Gideon a man of valor, a mighty warrior, even though he did not see himself that way. Gideon could not fathom that he would be a strong warrior to lead Israel to victory, but God made him victorious, and he ruled Israel for several years. God called Moses a leader, even though Moses thought of himself as a murderer and a poor orator. God saw Paul as the persecutor of sinfulness, even though Paul had been Saul, the persecutor of saints. He called Jacob *Israel*, when *Jacob* meant deceiver or trickster, as he'd tricked his brother, Esau, out of his birthright. He called Abram *Abraham*, which means "father of many nations." He renamed Abraham when he and his wife, Sarah, were old and unable to have children.

The only thing that should matter to you is what God calls you, not friends, family, or foe. And even if they call you by your reputation and not your identity, God is able to make everything new when you abide in Him. He is calling you to reveal His love and His purpose to you so that your life may be complete.

So what does purpose look like? How do you identify it? In simplest terms, it should look like Jesus. Our unique purpose is from our Creator and should embody Jesus; He should be at the core. Remember we discussed billions of sperm cells fighting to win the prize of being born into this world, our natural life? I believe that those other sperm may have carried purpose as well, but yours prevailed because it was more potent than the others. You won your natural life! The French priest and poet Pierre Teilard de Chardin stated, "We are not human beings having a spiritual experience; we are spiritual beings having a human experience."[76] What does that mean? That God made you in His image and likeness. God is spirit; therefore we are spirit. But we were put on this earth as spiritual beings to live naturally. Simply stated, if we live out our lives naturally, focusing on our flesh and the cares of this world, we disconnect ourselves from our Creator. But if we live in the Spirit, as Paul said in Galatians, then we should walk by the Spirit, not becoming boastful, challenging, and envying one another.[77] In fact, the preceding verse says that those who live in Christ Jesus (by the Spirit), have crucified their flesh with its passions and desires. So, we are to live according to the Spirit and the word of God, our Creator, operating at the core of our purpose, which is to serve others through. We don't have to hate others or be envious, because we beat out billions of competitors for our gift of life, just as they did. Our purpose may be different and unique in its context but similar in its content. We are to use our purpose to free others from the cares, stresses, and issues of this world, and serve and give of our talents, time, and treasures. Remember, we make a living by what we get; we make a life by what we give.

Chapter Five
The Training Ground

☙❧

"The purpose of life is to live it, to taste experience to the utmost, to reach out eagerly and without fear for newer and richer experience"

ELEANOR ROOSEVELT

"Until purpose is discovered, existence has no meaning. Fulfilling purpose must be the primary goal of every person."

DR. MYLES MUNROE

"The purpose of life is a life of purpose."

ROBERT BYRNE

"Here is the test to find whether your mission on earth is finished. If you're alive, it isn't."

RICHARD BACH

"The purpose of life is to live, and a life of purpose is worth not just living but dying for. Purpose gives us passion, which fuels us to live life to the fullest."

RICARDO A. RICHARDSON

Many of us understand the concept of practice makes perfect. If we've participated in sports, music, academics, or work, we've come across this statement on several occasions. We know that in order to get better at something we must practice it. Practice does make perfect, but it also makes permanent. If you practice good habits, you develop permanent ones. Likewise, if you practice bad habits, you develop the propensity to continue permanently in those poor choices. The more time, effort, hard work, and dedication we put into anything, the more we get out of it and the better we perform. But, in order to become better at a skill, we need the wisdom of a coach or someone considered a professional in the field to guide us.

Think of the times you had an issue with your vehicle. Who did you call? I'm sure it wasn't the maintenance man, but an auto mechanic who is skilled and trained in that field. When you feel sick you go to a doctor or a specialist. God is a general practitioner, but He is also a specialist because He is able to treat us generally and specifically based on our need.

A coach instructs us, trains us, and molds us until we succeed at the task at hand. For the athlete, the training ground is a sports field or court. For the scholar, it is the classroom. This is also true in life. God is our coach. He instructs us through His words, trains us and molds us into what we were intended to be. Life is the training ground used to bring out the purpose in each of us. God uses this principle to show us that there is a formula in life, and it requires us to put in time to study, train, and be dedicated to perfecting that which we want to accomplish. God's word is our instruction manual, perfecting us to operate in the potency of our purpose. God says that He will "equip you with everything good that you may do his will, working in you that which is pleasing in his sight."[78] Practice makes perfect, and God will perfect us in every good work, but we must also practice good works, faith, and learning about the Creator and His works.

To face the challenges of life, we need to study God's word and meditate on it so that we will always be prepared. Remember how you prepared for various subjects in school? If you studied, did your homework, and read the chapters ahead of the teacher, you were prepared for pop quizzes and exams. If you did not study, you failed. Life is God's training ground, and He tests us to see whether we know the subject, His word, and whether we will pass or fail in life. God doesn't tempt anyone, but He does test us.[79] Life is our classroom, and we need to know God's word to pass whatever test and trials we face. Relying on His word will reveal our purpose, which will propel us to a successful, fulfilling life.

When a king passes a law, all the citizens are required and expected to obey. Jesus is King of kings and Lord of lords. The word *king* means ruler; *lord* means owner. So Jesus is the Ruler of those that rule, and the Owner of those who own! Before the world, the Word (Christ) was. The Word was with God and became flesh and dwelt among us.[80] God's word is true and sharper than any double-edged sword. It fine-tunes, and it is useful to rebuke, reproof, build, and shape our lives. You live by it, and then you feast on its fruits. God's word will continue to renew our minds and give us fresh, new perspectives as well as His thoughts, desires, and will for our lives. May our eyes be opened to see His clear revelations as He reveals His mysteries to us—the mystery of our existence!

In addition to studying the words of the One who created us, we need to believe and have faith in those words. We can't plan our way through life outside of God's word, because the plan is contained in the purpose, and the purpose is in the Creator. God's ultimate purpose was to send Jesus to ensure that our purpose is revealed through Him. Your plan lies in the ultimate purpose of the Creator. How did Joseph know how to run Potiphar's house? How did he know how to run a prison? How was he able to interpret dreams and work for high-ranking officers and Pharaoh? His plans lay in his purpose!

Jesus came to earth as the purpose of God to redeem humanity, and He had the plan within Him. The plan and purpose became one in the person of Jesus Christ. Whatever you feel is impossible *is* impossible...by your own plan. But with God, nothing is impossible, because His plans are in His purpose. You can't effectively plan your life without going to God first. Seek first the kingdom of heaven and ALL things will be added to you.[81] *All* includes all purposes and all plans. Your only plan should be to seek God! That's it! His purpose will contain the plan for your life. The plans and purpose lie in God, the Creator.

Understand that the Creator's plan and purpose are one and the same! When you worry, you depend on your mind and your plan. When you can't figure out the answer to your own plan, worry, confusion, and uncertainty set in. The answers to life do not lie in your plans or mind but in your spirit, which must be connected to the Creator. He says to renew your mind, because all plans outside of God are vain, and He knows that the plans of a mind not renewed are not built on a solid foundation and will not be influenced by purpose. You cannot plan in your mind, but in your spirit and your purpose! In order to get the ultimate plan for your life, you have to get the plan of universal life: Jesus Christ! He is the Life and the Way, and no one comes to the Creator but by Him. When you understand His plan and His purpose, you will understand your plan and your purpose.

God will test our faith. If you ask God to be a healer, you have to have faith to believe He can heal you. When we go deeper into God to find our purpose, we must be prepared to face our fears, doubts, and own selfish plans because these things oppose His purpose. In order for light to shine, darkness must be present. Faith will overcome our doubt, and purpose will overcome our plans. How does God prove our faith? God knows the answer to the question before

He asks. He asks not for Himself but for our own hearing and understanding. He asked Adam, "Where art thou?" He asked Moses, "What is that you have in your hand?" He asked Ezekiel, "Can these bones live?" He asked Peter, "Do you love me?" He asked Paul, "Why do you persecute me?" He asked the blind man, "Do you want to see?" He asks you and me the same questions: "Do you believe that I am able?" "Do you have the faith to believe?" He already knows the answers.

When Jesus cursed the fig tree, the disciples were amazed that it withered and died. Jesus asked them, "Where is your faith?" He repeatedly questioned the disciples on their faith or lack thereof. Jesus told Peter, "But I have prayed for you Simon that your faith may not fail."[82] Jesus understood that whatever Peter needed or wanted was activated by his faith. Once Peter's faith was strong, Jesus told him to go and encourage his friends. Jesus knows that you and I are praying for the revelation of what our lives mean, but we need faith to be the agent that precedes the revelation. Life is the canvas on which to activate your faith. It is the training ground to grow in faith. Life is filled with doubt; what we see discourages us. But the word says we walk by faith and not by what we see.[83] Issues such as sickness in mind, body, and soul occur throughout life. It is not just a result of sin or what we have done; it exists as a training battleground for your faith. Faith is that confident assurance of what we know is going to happen. It is the evidence of things not seen.[84]

There was a blind man who came to Jesus, and the disciples asked what sin the man had committed to cause the blindness. They believed his disease was a result of something wicked he or his father had done. Jesus told them it was neither. This suggests that our ill conditions are not always connected to something we have done, but to the fact that life will bring situations that cast doubt, and it is the training ground that will empower you through faith! Life brings sickness to our mind, body, and soul so that we can believe God for our own healing. When life brings sickness or trials, we pray harder and seek God more diligently and exercise our faith. God demonstrated his power to everyone by waiting for Lazarus to be in the grave for four days, beyond the time when the body deteriorates. He wanted there to be no doubt that faith can manifest the power of God, and the greater the faith, the more miraculous the result. Jesus had so much faith that when He prayed for something, He did it with thanksgiving, because He already knew it would be done.

I attended high school at St. Augustine's College (SAC), a college preparatory school in Nassau, Bahamas. I was popular because I played sports, but I also matriculated through difficult classes like advanced mathematics and physics. I now understand why I operated on both sides of the track, befriending both the brainy kids and the jocks. I was a natural athlete, but my main love was for basketball. I did well in track and field but never practiced. I remember our principal, Mr. Leviticus (Lou) Adderley, as a no-nonsense principal who demanded only the best from his students in all areas both academically and athletically. Even as school principal, it seemed as if Mr. Adderley was involved in all areas of the students' lives. I believed that my ability to excel in sports and the fact that my grandmother, Agnes Richardson, was the religion teacher at the school gave me an advantage if I would ever get into trouble. Mr. Adderley challenged that belief when I got into a fight at school. Instead of detention, I reported to his office. He gave me several options to consider, one of which was to report to him on my behavioral progress and become more active in other sports, specifically track and field. I absolutely dreaded track because I didn't think it was a "cool" sport, plus you had to wear these small, tight shorts, which I thought was not good for my reputation around campus. Mr. Adderley gave me an ultimatum: Run track or be banned from playing basketball. This was an easy choice for me. I decided that I would run track, but I would not train; I'd only go through the motions during track practice. I ran the hurdles and was able to defeat every opponent at the school in my division.

My mother, Carolyn, was a member of the Bahamas Track & Field Association, and to this day still travels with the various teams to the Carifta Games, Olympics, and other track meets supporting Bahamian athletes. There was a track meet against other high schools, and my mother was there as a finish-line judge. I was confident that I could compete with the other schools because I dominated at my school. I ran the race and got beat in a photo finish against a student from a public high school known for its celebrated track athletes. The photo-finish picture was in the sports section of the local newspaper. My mother was so proud of me that day, but I felt like I cheated her, myself, and my teammates because I hadn't trained for that race. No one else knew that fact, but I did. The second-place finish was not something I coveted because I knew I had not given my best. If I had, I am sure I would have felt differently. I made a promise that day to always practice and train as hard as I could and take the advice of the coach who was there to develop and perfect my skills. I learned that you might do well if you fix your mistakes, but you do better if you learn from them.

I took this lesson with me to college and into my profession as an actuary. When I did not know how to develop a forecast or figure out adverse insurance claim losses of an insured group, I would spend late nights studying so that I would be on top of my game. If I got beat at anything, it would not be because I had not prepared or done my best, it would be because the other person was better that day. What I realized is that by not training to do your best to succeed, you are training to fail. Each of us should train to be the best at what we do. This may mean physical practice or mental practice through studying and education. These good habits can only develop and enhance the potency of our purpose.

Joseph practiced his visionary and leadership skills as a young boy and was committed to serving men of authority as he served God. He honored Potiphar, the prison warden, and Pharaoh prior to becoming the governor of the country. He practiced honesty, devotion, hard work, and commitment to service. Because he practiced them, these traits developed and enhanced his potency in serving his purpose as second-in-command to Pharaoh and providing salvation to his father's house and his people. God uses life's events, whether successes or trials, to train us in fulfilling our purpose, which can bring life or death through obedience or disobedience. God saw this in the people of Israel. They were practicing everything He told them not to, and so they were training themselves to be skilled in doing evil and wrong. Unfortunately, their practice brought severe judgment from the omniscient, omnipotent God.

God spoke to the prophet Jeremiah about Israel's unfaithfulness. The people were doing things other than what God wanted for them. God declared, "They are skilled in doing evil; they know not how to do good."[85] God is talking here about the result of the people's training. The people of Israel were worshiping foreign gods and practicing detestable things. In order for us to understand the kingdom of God, the Bible relates it to natural relationships, as with the parables Jesus taught. Jesus taught us how to relate to God and how to understand the kingdom of God with our limited knowledge by explaining earthly parables with kingdom principles. We see that in Jeremiah. The bond between mankind and God is a covenant likened to marriage. The Bible often refers to God's people as His bride, and the Israelites' adultery was unfaithfulness in serving God as they committed themselves to serving idols. The evidence of this is given in Jeremiah, when God asks him,

Have you seen what faithless Israel has done? She has gone up to every high hill and under every spreading tree and has committed adultery there. I thought that after she had done all this she would return to me but she did not, and her unfaithful sister Judah saw it. I gave faithless Israel her certificate of divorce and sent her away because of all her adulteries. Yet I saw that her unfaithful sister Judah had no fear; she also went out and committed adultery.[86]

This is evidence that God saw that Israel was immoral and defiled the land by committing adultery with stone and wood; in other words, worshiping that which was made by man's hands is idolatry. God had every right to divorce them, but later declared that Israel should return to Him and He would forgive her. This is a valuable lesson for us, as God uses our lives as a training ground for us to overcome and succeed. God knew Israel's desire to worship, serve, and love, but they were serving creation and not the Creator, worshiping "every high hill and under every spreading tree."

Many people look to love and serve another but focus on the wrong man or woman. They sow love, but in the wrong field, just as the people of God sowed their love in the wrong field, worshiping idols instead of God. The discipline to love and serve God will only enhance the revelation of your purpose.

The Bible says that we should look to the hill—God's holy hill Mount Zion—for our strength. The people of Israel were looking up to the hill, but it was not the hill of the Creator, it was a hill of their own desire. What is your hill? Have you made your own desires your hill? Is it a person in your life or a relationship? Is it your money? Your reputation? If your heart is set on the wrong hill, as were the people of Israel, you won't be able to receive the revelation of your purpose, or any spiritual revelation for that matter.

The people also were not only looking at the wrong father, but to the wrong son. They were looking toward the hills, every spreading tree, and the sun. In other words, they were looking at everything in creation for the answer to their problems. The metaphor here is that God is the holy hill and his son, Jesus, is the spreading tree. Jesus Christ was sent to save the lost—an adulterous nation—and He died on a tree on Calvary with his arms spread out. He is described as the Tree of Life and was the spreading tree that the people of Israel should have been looking toward. The people of Israel were looking to the future but to the wrong spreading tree! If you are to have your life defined and your purpose developed, you need to look to the right coach, the right mentor, the true Creator, and the right Spreading Tree.

Faithfulness is very important in developing your purpose on life's training ground, because it requires the belief that God will not only reveal your purpose, but will mentor you and birth it through you. We learn from the people of Israel that faithlessness is equated with adultery toward God. The Bible says, "And without faith it is impossible to please God, because anyone who comes to him must believe that he exists and he rewards those who earnestly seek him."[87]

Faith activates God to reward you, to reveal your purpose to you, as you earnestly seek Him. Faith is a powerful tool. It allows you to lean not on your understanding or knowledge but on God's existence. We have to first believe that God exists so that He can show us why *we* exist! God understands our longing to know ourselves and our lifelong purpose, the reason we were born. His reward to us is to first rid us of our wandering minds and bewilderment, then give us the surety that we exist for a singular and universal purpose: to have an impact on His kingdom on earth.

I am amazed at the athletes who play professional sports. They have dedicated their lives to that particular sport and make what is difficult look easy. They participate at a high level so effortlessly. Michael Jordan was one of the greatest basketball players who ever played the game, although my thirteen-year-old son, Zion, believes that Kobe Bryant eventually will be known as a better player than Michael Jordan. I disagree with him, as I am his coach and know more than he does, but that's another subject. What I do agree with is that both men dedicated themselves to practicing and becoming great among other professionals. They have a term for this: superstars. These superstars have elevated their game above the best in the game, the stars. They are considered the crème de la crème.

The Michael Jordan story is well known. He played basketball for Laney High School in Wilmington, North Carolina, and was, ironically, cut from the varsity team as a sophomore. Instead of giving up after being cut from the team, Jordan took it as a personal challenge to achieve greater things, practicing for hours on the basketball court. He understood that in order to develop his talent he would have to train and put in the work. He once said, "Whenever I was working out and got tired and figured I ought to stop, I'd close my eyes and see that list in the locker room without my name on it, and that usually got me going again."[88] Jordan eventually made the team and led it to the state championship. He did not give up but dedicated his life to the game. He practiced continually until he became better than most people who ever played the game. He went on to become a superstar and champion, winning six NBA championship titles.

Just as Jordan worked hard at becoming "skilled" in his sport, so we are to develop our gifts and skills for the kingdom of God. In the face of challenge and adversity, purpose can be revealed and realized. It is your Creator's job to reveal the reason you exist as you seek Him, and it is your job to prepare and develop yourself. Many of us are just beginning our training in life, and others are just a few steps away from living in our purpose. Whatever we do in life, we should make a positive difference in the lives of others. We are to serve others as Jesus served us. Some may believe that Jordan's only purpose was to play basketball, but there is life after basketball. His life may have influenced other young ball players to learn the hard lesson of commitment and hard work, and these are great lessons for all of us. But I believe we can go deeper in our purpose. As I've said before, our life's purpose is not to gain position, but our position helps us gain purpose. Jordan has the position and stature in life to influence young people by teaching lessons other than how to bounce a basketball. Whether he embraces that to instill positive values in his fans and followers is another matter.

I love the game of basketball and am entertained by the athletes, but what I love most about the NBA is an initiative that gives it purpose. NBA Cares is an outreach initiative where each of the NBA teams and individual stars venture into the community to help others. They provide a helping hand and support to many who need it, fans or not. During each broadcast, you see one of the players talking about what he has done in the community and how he is making an impact. Some may say that this is only to bring good publicity to the league, but they are doing good, which is what God calls us all to do.

God calls us to be skilled in the good things we do. In other words, we are to develop good qualities so that we can teach others to be good and to do well. God wants us not to grow weary in doing good. God said to Jeremiah, "My people are skilled in doing evil, they know not how to do good."[89] In order to be skilled, you have to practice consistently and continually. God said that the people of Israel were skilled in doing what He did not want them to do. They were not using life as a training ground for their purpose; they were developing the wrong skills. The psalmist wrote, "Blessed is the man who does not walk in the counsel of the wicked or stand in the way of sinners or sit in the seat of mockers. But his delight is in the law of the Lord, and on his law he meditates day and night. He is like a tree planted by streams of water, which yields its fruit in season and whose leaf does not wither. Whatever he does prospers."[90] What an awesome promise! But don't miss the most important point: Do not walk, stand, or sit in sin. Why does the writer point out these physical movements? Because when you walk down the wrong path or with the wrong crowd, you are at the beginning stages of practicing and becoming skilled at the wrong things, namely sin.

Many of us search our minds as we contemplate sin. We think about doing something wrong and what consequences it might bring. We wonder, "How will we benefit? Who will know?" This is the stage of walking. The Bible says, "Enter through the narrow gate. For wide is the gate and broad is the road that leads to destruction, and many enter through it. But small is the gate and narrow the road that leads to life and only a few find it."[91] The narrow (straight) gate means that one must come in the narrower way of the gate in order to reach the path that leads to eternal life. This path is the path of choosing Jesus Christ and serving Him.

We are called to walk on the path of righteousness and not destruction. Once we begin walking on the road to sin or destruction, the tendency is to stay on that road. The psalmist begins with a man who does not walk in the way of the wicked, stand in the way of sinners, or sit in the seat of the mockers. He understands that when you stand close to sin, you are becoming a little more comfortable in that sinful situation. Curiosity or ignorance may have led you down the wrong path, but now your desire to do wrong becomes stronger, and you begin to stand around. You may not be physically participating, but you are spiritually and emotionally participating. Then finally you take a seat because you have become comfortable in that wrong situation. God warns us about becoming enticed by sin and sitting in it. We are to train ourselves in the things of God, because not training is a choice to operate in those things that will not reveal God's plan for our lives.

Many of us fall prey to the notion that we stumble into sin or fall into bad habits. In some cases, disease is hereditary, but some diseases are developed over time. An alcoholic may develop a dependency on alcohol. The American Medical Association defines alcoholism as a primary, chronic disease with genetic, psychosocial, and environmental factors influencing its development and manifestations. The disease is often progressive and fatal. It is characterized by impaired control over drinking, preoccupation with alcohol, use of alcohol despite adverse consequences, and distortions in thinking, most notably denial.[92] Notice the words *impaired,* or lack of control over drinking, and *denial.* The alcoholic is comfortable with drinking and is in denial that it is controlling his life. In other words, he is comfortable in his situation, sitting in alcoholism, not testing it out to see its affects; it has already manifested its effect on his life.

This is a practical lesson for us to do well and practice the right things so that we become skilled in our life. Walk, stand, and sit in those things that will bring life to us, not death. When you seek and fear God, says King Solomon, this is the beginning of wisdom.[93] Then you will have a desire to become more knowledgeable about God and about life. You will develop an attitude of excellence in everything you do. You are now training the correct way. You are developing the right attitude and right disposition for purpose to take you to your rightful position.

As the people of Israel were warned, they were practicing bad habits. They were practicing sin; in fact, they became "skilled" at it. God wants us to become skilled at doing His work, skilled at following His commandments, skilled about learning His word, and skilled about our commitment to seeking Him. The Bible says, "Study and be eager and do your utmost to present yourself to God approved (tested by trial), a workman who has no cause to be ashamed, correctly analyzing and accurately dividing [rightly handling and skillfully teaching] the Word of Truth."[94]

In order to experience our true existence, we need to seek God, study His word, and understand the application of it to our lives. This truth, along with the faith to apply what you hear and know about God, will be the tools you need to experience your purpose in God. The good news is that God can turn around your situation even if you have started on the wrong path and have been developing bad habits into permanent ones that have influenced your character. The French poet Jean de La Fontaine said, "A person often meets his destiny on the road he took to avoid it."[95] But in order to meet your destiny on the wrong road, you have to be in the right mind, seeking God. God can reveal to you your purpose even if you are on the wrong road; that revelation will allow you to embrace your purpose and get on the correct path to live a fruitful and fulfilling life.

Moses was an example of meeting his destiny and his purpose even though he took a detour. The Bible tells the story of how the king of Egypt wanted to execute all the newborn boys so that he could limit a fast-growing Hebrew population. The story tells the birth of Moses and how his mother hid him to save his life. After he could no longer be hidden, his mother took a papyrus basket, placed Moses in it, and pushed it among the reeds along the bank of the Nile River. His sister, Miriam, meanwhile, watched from a distance to see what would happen to her baby brother. As she watched, Pharaoh's daughter approached the Nile to bathe and noticed the basket among the reeds. She retrieved the basket, discovered the baby crying, and felt sorry for him. The Bible says she noticed that Moses was a Hebrew baby. Miriam immediately came forward and asked the princess if she wanted her to find a Hebrew woman to nurse the baby. After the princess agreed, Miriam went and brought his own mother to nurse him. When the child grew older, his mother took him to the princess, and he became her son. Pharaoh's daughter named him Moses, saying, "I drew him out of water."[96]

The story goes on to tell about Moses coming to the rescue of one of his Hebrew brothers. He saw an Egyptian mistreating a Hebrew and he killed the Egyptian in defense. After word got to Pharaoh about what Moses did, Pharaoh sought to harm Moses for committing murder against an Egyptian.

Even as a child, Moses had a purpose, as we all do. His purpose was to deliver the Hebrew people. Life offered the child the first opportunity when his mother sent him down the Nile River to protect his life. Moses began his purpose by delivering his sister and mother. When Pharaoh's daughter found Moses, she needed someone to nurse him, and it ended up being his own mother. Not only did Moses' mother get to nurse her own child, she was paid to do so! As a child, Moses became the prince of Egypt, the very nation that was enslaving his people. God used Moses' life as a training ground to deliver his purpose. He delivered Miriam and mother as a baby, then as a young prince he delivered the Hebrew from an Egyptian. Moses was a deliverer from birth, as this was his purpose. Moses grew up as an Egyptian in Pharaoh's palace and knew everything about the Egyptians. God trained him to fulfill his purpose.

The Bible tells about the encounter that Moses had with God. Moses tried to run away from his destiny and purpose, but God brought him right back to Egypt to face Pharaoh and demand the release of the Israelites. Destiny is that place where only purpose can take you. Moses knew his identity of purpose as a deliverer, and no matter which road he planned to pursue, purpose brought him to the place destined for him. God told Moses that he would deliver the people by

His hand. Moses, still running from his purpose, told God, "I have never been eloquent, neither in the past nor since you have spoken to your servant. I am slow of speech and tongue."[97] In today's language, Moses might have said, "I did not do well in school; I failed Language Arts, and I flunked speech class." He gave God excuses why he could not operate in his purpose. What excuses have you been making? Not enough education? You don't come from the right family or background? You're of the wrong race or ethnicity?

Look at what God says about excuses. He tells Moses, "Who gave human beings their mouths? Who makes them deaf or mute? Who gives them sight or makes them blind? Is it not I, the Lord? Now go; I will help you speak and will teach you what to say."[98] God will not only reveal your purpose, He will help you fulfill it. He said that He would never leave you nor forsake you. You can depend on your Creator to stand by you and help deliver and fulfill that which you were designed to do. As God spoke to Moses, so He speaks to us. We don't need to make excuses about our inadequacies and weakness; God will develop us or use others to enhance and deliver our purpose. God assures you that while you have been searching all your life for your purpose, He has it in His hands and wants to reveal it to you and teach you all you need to know to fulfill it. As He told Moses, He wants to teach you what to say, what to do, and how to live out your purpose!

David also used life as a training ground for his purpose. When Samuel anointed David king, even though he was just a boy and would not rule for several years, God gave him power. God revealed David's purpose to him as a young shepherd boy. David would watch over all his family's sheep, both great and small. Later he would watch and protect the sheep of Israel as their king. David knew who he was, because God called him king.

While still a young boy, the Philistine army came to fight against the Israelites. Their champion, Goliath, stood nine feet tall and taunted the Israelites. Saul, Israel's king, and all of his men were terrified. Goliath challenged that if any Israelite could defeat him, the Philistines would be their servants. David heard this and accepted the challenge.[99]

David had trained to fight by killing a bear and a lion and saw Goliath as someone opposing God and therefore opposing him. Saul offered David the same protection that Goliath had, namely a tunic, coat of armor, and a helmet. But David could not function naturally in the protection of man, only of God. God provided David with all the provision his purpose would need to prevail. David needed only a sling and small stones to defeat the Philistine giant. And defeat him he did.

This reminds me of how we approach the giants in our lives. We put on the armor of men, such as the helmet and various defenses, which are the very chains that constrain us just as they did young David. We are unable to walk around or function naturally because we come against problems, issues, obstacles, and challenges in our life with our own armor as opposed to the armor of God. David understood that in order to defeat his giant, he needed to put on the armor of God, not Saul's armor.

Finally, be strong in the Lord and in his mighty power. Put on the full armor of God so that you can take your stand against the devil's schemes. For our struggle is not against flesh and blood, but against the rulers, against the authorities, against the powers of this dark world and against the spiritual forces of evil in the heavenly realms. Therefore put on the full armor of God, so that when the day of evil comes, you may be able to stand your ground, and after you have done everything, to stand. Stand firm then, with the belt of truth buckled around your waist, with the breastplate of righteousness in place, and with your feet fitted with the readiness that comes from the gospel of peace. In addition to all this, take up the shield of faith, with which you can extinguish all the flaming arrows of the evil one. Take the helmet of salvation and the sword of the Spirit, which is the word of God.[100]

When we put on the penetrable armor of men, we expose ourselves to danger. But when we put on the impenetrable armor of God, we protect ourselves from all harm. David realized that belief in God, along with a slingshot and small stones, gave him more protection than Saul's armor and helmet.

God gave David power over fear when Samuel anointed him king. He trusted God when he faced the lion and the bear and knew God would deliver him from Goliath. David knew that his purpose would be protected as it had been by God from his youth. Throughout David's life, God would train and develop him to reveal his purpose, which was to protect and watch over God's people. All we need to do is look back on our lives to see how God has shown up in our situations to protect us from hurt, harm, and danger. If we reflect on our lives, we will see that protection was there for our purpose. Just as David's life was a training ground, so are yours and mine. God is developing you and I so that our purpose can achieve its full potency. God is the same yesterday, today, and forever. He still reveals purpose, gives provision, and protects it.

Chapter Six
Your Weapon Is Formed

୧୨

"But I have raised you up for this very purpose, that I might show you my power and that my name might be proclaimed in all the earth."

EXODUS 9:16 NIV

"The beloved of the Lord shall dwell in safety by him; and the Lord shall cover him all the day long."

DEUTERONOMY 33:12 KJV

"Our plans expose us to danger when positioned behind the penetrable armor of man, but purpose positions us behind the impenetrable armor of God."

RICARDO A. RICHARDSON

God is a God of purpose, and He has purpose in everything He does and everything He creates. God doesn't make mistakes. When He created man and earth, He called it good. He knew that everything in creation, including man, was good, and it was weaved together by His hand. God created purpose and destiny. In order for destiny to be fulfilled, purpose has to be revealed and implemented. Purpose is the gift, and destiny is the result of the gift. God gives His gift of purpose as He gives the gift of life. But just as others want to destroy your life, so they want to destroy your purpose. You have to protect it. How? Position yourself behind the impenetrable armor of your Creator.

God's divine purpose given to Jesus for the created world was to redeem the lost and sinful man to Him. Jesus said, reading from the book of Isaiah, "The Spirit of the Lord is upon me, for he has anointed me to bring good news to the poor ... He has sent me to proclaim that captives will be released, that the blind will see, that the oppressed will be set free."[101] He also said, "I have come that they may have life and they may have it more abundantly."[102] God wants you to have life in abundance, in full measure, and that means living the life you were destined to live. We can only have abundant life by living in the core. Living outside of God in the slices of life may allow you to exist, but according to Jesus, it will not be an abundant spiritual life. Jesus was the ultimate gift to humanity, with the ultimate purpose to ensure that your purpose is revealed, manifested, and executed. We truly cannot have life without having purpose. His purpose was to ensure that we have a life of purpose, just as He did. We don't need to settle in life, going about our daily chores, falling into a rut. We can find true happiness and fulfillment because Jesus purposed it that way.

Like any parent, Mary was very protective of her son, Jesus. She was highly favored among women because she would carry the seed that would deliver humanity. I wonder, who did people say that Mary was? God called her highly favored, the only time such a description appears in the Bible. I could imagine what other people were saying about Mary. She was engaged to be married and found pregnant. They probably called her unfaithful, immoral, and unworthy of Joseph. But Mary knew what God said about her and all the promises He made to her, because she said to the angel, "Be it unto me, according to thy word."[103] Mary's purpose was to carry the Promise of Salvation to humanity and give birth to the Promise. Her process was the exact process we all must go through to birth our purpose.

Dr. Myles Munroe, gifted author and pastor, spoke about *Life Lessons From the Incarnation* during a teaching session at Bahamas Faith Ministries in Nassau, Bahamas, in December 2008. I was fortunate to be there that morning to receive a prophecy from him about my purpose in life. He informed me that he would mentor me; that he would be my Elizabeth, whose birth of John the Baptist was an example of God's ability to do the impossible. Elizabeth's experience of having a baby in old age was also an example to Mary that God can do what He purposes, regardless of what man thinks.

God does not worry about our circumstances. Mary was engaged to Joseph, but because she found favor with God, He gave her the specific purpose of being the mother of the Christ. God could have chosen Elizabeth. She was a descendant of Aaron. The Bible says that she and her husband, Zechariah, a priest, were upright in the sight of God, observing all of the Lord's commandments and regulations blamelessly.[104] But God had another purpose for Elizabeth, one that would precede Mary's. The angel told Mary about Elizabeth, who was said to be barren but pregnant in her old age, for nothing is impossible with God. Mary needed an example of God doing impossible things, and her example was Elizabeth. In fact, Elizabeth's purpose was to birth John, the harbinger who was to declare the way before Jesus. John prepared the way for Jesus, and Elizabeth prepared a way for Mary.

When Mary received her purpose through God's promise, she had trouble believing it because she was looking through a worldly lens. The "facts" said she was a virgin and her cousin was barren and beyond child-birthing years. But our Creator always looks at things through spiritual or supernatural lenses, which is why He declares that His ways and thoughts are higher than ours. He knows the end at the beginning, "declaring the end from the beginning, and from ancient times things that are not yet done, saying, 'My counsel shall stand, and I will do all My pleasure.'"[105] God will do His pleasure and his purpose whether or not we receive it. If we refuse, He will find someone who is willing to say, as Mary did, "Be it unto me just as you have said." It is in our best interest to get in the position for God to use us as He did Elizabeth and Mary.

Mary's purpose, like the purpose of everyone we have read about, was pursuing her. Your purpose was assigned to you by God and will continue to pursue you until you accept it. Mary did what most of us need to do when God reveals our purpose to us: accept it just as it was said. When Mary got the word from the angel, she immediately left to visit Elizabeth. She did not hesitate. Has God been speaking to you? Have you been feeling your purpose pursuing you? Do you feel a pulling at your heart to give of yourself to some noble cause connected to the Creator and His kingdom? Do you feel a calling to do something different than what you have done before?

Mary responded to the call and began the process that we all must go through. She believed God and exercised her faith. She continued to perfect her belief by staying with Elizabeth, standing in her presence, and then sitting at her feet. She learned that Elizabeth had already experienced what she was about to go through—the morning sickness, the cravings, and all the issues of childbirth. Mary became skilled at developing her purpose so that she could give birth to that purpose. The Bible says that when Elizabeth heard Mary's greeting, the baby leaped in her womb, and Elizabeth was filled with the Holy Spirit. In a loud voice she exclaimed, "Blessed are you among women, and blessed is the child you will bear! But why am I so favored, that the mother of my Lord should come to me? As soon as the sound of your greeting reached my ears, the baby in my womb leaped for joy. Blessed is she who has believed that the Lord would fulfill his promises to her!"[106]

God called Mary highly favored, and now Elizabeth was favored because Mary had come to her. The purpose and favor of God is so potent that it will be experienced by those around you. Elizabeth felt blessed that the presence of God was in her house. Do you realize that there may be greatness and royalty right in your house? Nurture and encourage those in your life so that they can focus on God, who can reveal a royal purpose in their lives. And He will do the same for you! Mary had an example to follow in Elizabeth, someone who believed God and had her purpose revealed and manifested by God.

Mary gave birth to her purpose, but now she had to protect it. People will try to abort your dreams, your promises, and your purpose while you are still carrying it within you. You have to be prayerful, faithful, and persistent in delivering it. After Jesus was born, the Bible tells how Herod sought to kill the baby. Herod pretended that he wanted to seek out Jesus to worship Him, but he really wanted to destroy God's Purpose. Joseph was instructed in a dream to take Mary and Jesus and escape to Egypt. The word of God says that they lived in Egypt until Herod died and could no longer harm them or the Purpose for humanity in their care.

God created and wired us to be dependent on Him. Who we are and what we have are gifts from God. Who of us were able to select our mother or father? Our parents were given to us by the Creator, and we were entrusted to them for a time. You did not create yourself, so how can you know what you are supposed to do? How can you know your purpose? It is impossible for you to determine what your purpose is outside of your Creator. If equipment is not performing as it should, we say that it has malfunctioned. Many of us are malfunctioning every day because we are trying to function on our own accord, as if we created ourselves. We are, in essence, out of the right function in our lives, our jobs, our relationships, and our marriages. And we wonder why our lives are so dysfunctional!

Our Creator has the true functionality for each of us. Because He understands how we each function properly, He is able to remove the dysfunction in our lives. God wants us to be dependent on Him so that we will function as we should, but the dependency on Him is our choice. We have to make the decision to trust God with our lives. We should allow Him to instruct us on living as we were created to do. He will give us all good gifts, including the gift of purpose and functionality.

If we look at this from an inventor's standpoint, we get an understanding of how God, our inventor, views us. In order for the invention to fully function, it needs to be properly built by the inventor. Often the invention may need to be tweaked or repaired, and the most qualified repair person is the inventor. But God created us perfect. The psalmist realized this when he said, "I praise you; for I am fearfully and wonderfully made: marvelous are Your works; and that my soul knows very well."[107] When we rely on the Creator, He will refine us as He refines gold. He tweaks us back to perfection. As we go through life, we are continually tested and refined. It is our faith in the Creator that accelerates our refinement. Life is a training ground for purpose, and God is our Creator and our coach, refining us to be able to give birth and deliver our purpose to this world. He created us to be fully dependent on Him. We need Him to reveal our purpose for our lives, and then we need Him to help us give birth to it. We also need God to help protect our purpose so that it is fully manifested in our lives and the lives of others.

Mary was able to believe God, receive the promise, and give birth to her purpose. Herod wanted to kill God's purpose, and he sought the help of the magi or wise men. Just like Herod, there are people in our lives who will want to destroy our purpose, and if we do not protect it, they will succeed. Many of them may come to compliment and praise you, but in fact they want to do you harm. But God knows the end at the beginning, and if we depend on Him, He will direct our paths. He appeared to Joseph in a dream and warned him about Herod. The family fled to Egypt in the middle of the night, where they stayed until Herod's death. That is the potency of purpose! God will remove anyone or anything that stands in the way of your purpose being fulfilled!

Moses' purpose was protected from birth. He was adopted as a prince when Pharaoh's daughter found him in a basket on the riverbank. Although he lived a life of luxury in Egypt, his purpose was ever present. The time for its manifestation happened when Moses defended a Hebrew from an attack by an Egyptian and killed him. As a result, he had to flee to save his own life. But the power of Moses' purpose continued to grow to the point where he returned to face Pharaoh and demand the release of God's people. This was a bold move, as Moses was on the Egyptian Most Wanted list. Not only was Moses' purpose protecting his life but also the life of all the Israelites under slavery in Egypt. The final act of protection came when Pharaoh and his entire army vigorously pursued Moses and the

Israelites to enslave or destroy them. God stepped in and miraculously delivered Moses and protected his purpose, which was the exodus out of Egypt.

Moses and the people were successful in their physical exodus out of Egypt, but they failed in the mental and spiritual exodus. While they escaped Pharaoh and were physically free, they remained in mental bondage, worshiping idols made with their own hands, as opposed to the God that had given them their freedom.

Moses' purpose in leading the people would be passed down to Joshua, a new leader for a new generation. Joshua's purpose protected him throughout his life, as he was a great "warrior of faith." He consulted his God before he entered battle and achieved victory. He successfully led his generation into the land promised to his and Moses' generations. He believed God and acted on faith. Joshua's name in the Hebrew is translated "salvation" or "to be victorious" and "to deliver and be liberated." His name stood for freedom, liberation, and salvation. That was his purpose, and his purpose protected him and delivered his people.

Even though Moses' purpose didn't deliver him to see the promise land, his relative, Caleb, did. We see the story of Caleb recorded in Joshua:

Now the people of Judah approached Joshua at Gilgal, and Caleb, son of Jephunneh the Kenizzite said to him, "You know what the Lord said to Moses the man of God at Kadesh Barnea about you and me. I was forty years old when Moses the servant of the Lord sent me from Kadesh Barnea to explore the land. And I brought him back a report according to my convictions, but my fellow Israelites who went up with me made the hearts of the people melt in fear. I, however, followed the Lord my God wholeheartedly. So on that day Moses swore to me, 'The land on which your feet have walked will be your inheritance and that of your children forever, because you have followed the Lord my God wholeheartedly.' Now then, just as the Lord promised, he has kept me alive for forty-five years since the time he said this to Moses, whil Israel moved about in the wilderness. So here I am today, eighty-five years old! I am still as strong today as the day Moses sent me out; I'm just as vigorous to go out to battle now as I was then. Now give me this hill country that the Lord promised me that day. You yourself heard then that the Anakites were there and their cities were large and fortified, but, the Lord helping me, I will drive them out just as he said." Then Joshua blessed Caleb son of Jephunneh and gave him Hebron as his inheritance. So Hebron has belonged to Caleb son of Jephunneh the Kenizzite ever since, because he followed the Lord, the God of Israel, whole-heartedly.[108]

Caleb followed God's blueprint for life and God's word. He didn't have the complete written word in the Bible like you and I have, but he listened to the words God spoke to Moses and through His commandments. Caleb was eighty-five years old when the power of his purpose was manifested. We are never too old to receive our purpose from God once we decide to follow him wholeheartedly.

The lessons that Moses and Mary teach us are how to be impregnated with purpose and protect and deliver it. Mary simply lived a life acceptable to God and was favored by Him, so He revealed the divine purpose to her. The divine purpose of the Christ is the most important of mankind, and that is the redemption of sins. The lesson here is that we should allow God to reveal our purpose and seek to serve Him. The prophet Isaiah spoke of the birth of Jesus long before Mary's existence. Her purpose to participate in the delivery of Jesus was sent from God before Mary was born. The meaning of her existence was revealed to her regarding the birth of the Savior of the world. She believed what was revealed to her and began walking in that revelation. She was instructed to find someone who was also walking in purpose at a more mature stage than she. That person was her cousin, Elizabeth. Mary began her training with Elizabeth to be able to deliver her purpose. She followed in her footsteps and gave birth to Jesus. Although she successfully delivered her purpose, it still needed protection, but again, the Creator was the one who protects purpose from danger. As long as Mary walked in the purpose of God, she would be protected as well.

You and I must experience the exact same things that Mary did in order to be able to successfully deliver what God has destined for us. He will reveal it to you and then instruct you on how to carry it to full term before its birth. That is why it is so important to stay connected to the Creator. God's purpose for you is important to the world. That purpose pursued you even before you were conceived. In fact, it is the very reason that you were conceived. It drove you to beat out those billion other sperm cells and become victorious. You could have died in that pursuit, but you survived, and the fact that you are reading these words now proves that you are here for a reason.

If you do not yet know your purpose, you may feel frustrated. Ask your Creator to reveal your purpose to you. He has been protecting you all this time, waiting for you to ask Him to reveal it. The Bible says that if you ask, God will not withhold any good thing, especially the purpose for your life. Jesus said, "I tell you the truth, my Father will give you whatever you ask in my name. Until now you have not asked for anything in my name. Ask and you will receive, and your joy will be complete."[109] And again, James, the brother of Jesus, said, "You desire but do not have, so you kill. You covet but you cannot get what you want, so you quarrel and fight. You do not have because you do not ask God."[110] Ask God to plainly reveal your purpose and the meaning of your existence and He will. The only condition is that you have a relationship with Him as your Father and Creator. He will protect your purpose from adversaries and ensure that you fully operate and function in it.

Chapter Seven
The Fruits of Purpose

ᘐᘐ

"From the east I summon a bird of prey; from a far-off land, a man to fulfill my purpose. What I have said, that I will bring about; what I have planned, that I will do."

ISAIAH 46:11

"I have held many things in my hands and have lost them all. But whatever I have placed in God's hands, that I still possess."

MARTIN LUTHER

"God's word is His seed that when watered with our faith reaps a purpose in our lives."

RICARDO A. RICHARDSON

Growing up in the Bahamas, I loved the variety of native fruits, some you probably never heard of before. My favorites were mangoes, tamarinds, plums, jujus, guavas, and dillies. Whenever I wanted a snack, I would just climb a tree and pick the fruit. No matter the time of the year, there was always fruit in season. What a blessing it was to be able to eat all different types of fruits year round. The purpose of those trees was to produce fruit in their season. The mango tree produced fruit in its season, and so did the guavas and plums. The common driving force of each tree was purpose, although the seasons for the production of fruit were all different. When I left to study in the United States, I would come home to the Bahamas every Christmas holiday, and the first thing I asked was, "What fruit is in season?" If it was not the season for the fruit I wanted, I could not enjoy its blessings. But even if the tree currently was not bearing fruit, it did not mean that it was not operating within its intended purpose.

God designed the trees in such a way as to maximize their purpose and produce fruit in due season. Everything that the tree needs to fulfill its purpose, regardless of what kind of tree it is, is provided by its Creator. Likewise, everything that each person needs to fulfill his purpose is provided by his Creator. The tree produces fruit in its season; likewise man produces fruit in his season. The tree has seed within the fruit that when planted back into the soil (connected to God), reproduces again and again. The seed placed in each of us is the seed of purpose, and when we connect back to God, He gives us understanding about our purpose. This seed is placed deep within us, and it is the person of understanding who can draw the seed of purpose out so that it can produce its fruit in season.

The proverb states, "The purpose in a man's heart is like deep waters, but a man of understanding will draw it out."[111] The seed in man is also able to reproduce itself through his progeny, who in turn has the ability to reproduce both his purpose and himself. The Creator of trees, plants, animals, and man is the same. We were all created by God, and He gave a command as to how fruitful His creation would be. The Bible says that God proclaimed, "Let the land produce vegetation: seed-bearing plants and trees on the land that bear fruit with seed in it, according to their various kinds. And it was so. The land produced vegetation: plants bearing seed according to their kinds and trees bearing fruit with seed in it according to their kinds. And God saw that it was good."[112]

God gave us the gift of trees that bear various kinds of fruit, like mangoes, oranges, apples, cherries, plums, and all the other fruits we enjoy. But He also gave the trees a gift of purpose, which is to produce and reproduce fruit. Not only did God give them the gift of purpose, He also gave them the provisions for their purpose. Everything the tree needs to fulfill its purpose is given to it by its Creator. God provides sunlight, rain, and nutrients in the soil. These are essential provisions for a tree to live and produce fruit. God, in His infinite wisdom, created the tree to have its purpose be to produce fruit, but also to have a purpose to coexist with man. When God created vegetation, man, and earth, He said it was good. God connected us to the trees that produce the fruit as our sustenance through photosynthesis. Photosynthesis is the process in which trees use the energy from sunlight to produce sugar, which cellular respiration converts into adenosine triphosphate (ATP), a common form of energy (fuel) stored in all living systems. This is essentially the energy coin of the cell in living creatures. This energy is the plant's food, which contains glucose and oxygen. All of this seems like a brief chemistry lesson, but essentially the photosynthetic process uses water (rain from the Creator) and carbon dioxide and releases the oxygen that we breathe in every day. Here is the connection: The carbon dioxide that plants need comes from humans. We give them what they need to survive and they give us what we need to survive. And it all comes from the Creator.

A tree needs rain and radiance from the sun to grow and fulfill its purpose; so, too, man needs rain and the radiance of the Son to grow and fulfill his purpose. "The Son is the radiance of God's glory and the exact representation of his being, sustaining all things by his powerful word."[113] This verse sums up the essence of purpose and how it is sustained. Jesus is the Son of the living God, and He is the sustainer of all living things, both plant and man. In order for man to operate in his purpose, he needs the radiance of the Son to shine in his life because the Son is able to sustain us by His word. As the light comes from the Son of God, so does the rain. The rain for man is God's own Spirit, as stated by the prophet Joel, "I will pour out my Spirit on all people. Your sons and daughters will prophesy, your old men will dream dreams, your young men will see visions."[114]

Jesus also talks about living water that man needs in order to be sustained in life just as the rain sustains vegetation. On one occasion, Jesus asked a Samaritan woman for a drink from the well. She responded in disbelief because the Jews did not socialize let alone share water with Samaritans. But Jesus pressed on and told her that if she knew who was asking her for a drink, she would have asked him for living water. When she inquired as to where she would get living water, Jesus responded, "Everyone who drinks this water will be thirsty again, but whoever drinks the water I give them will never thirst. Indeed, the water I give them will become in them a spring of water welling up to eternal life."[115]

God created all creation with the same basic needs for water and light. He is the only one who can provide both water and light, either by the sun or the Son. God even speaks to man's seed and to his offspring. He told Isaiah, "For I will pour water upon him that is thirsty, and floods upon the dry ground: I will pour my spirit upon thy seed, and my blessing upon thine offspring."[116] As the trees and vegetation depend on their Creator to sustain them, so does man. Whenever a tree is uprooted from its natural habitat, it dies because the nutrients needed for its survival are in the soil. The tree is operating within the laws of its Creator, as He purposed the tree to thrive in the soil. Whenever you uproot a person from the word or laws of God, he loses the "nutrients" necessary for his survival and the establishment of the purpose for his life. Jesus said, "It is written: 'Man shall not live on bread alone, but on every word that comes from the mouth of God.'"[117]

So we have the same ingredients as plants to produce good fruit. Good fruit is that which is consumed to bring a positive outcome. When we eat good fruit, it helps our body fight against free radicals and other harmful elements. Similarly, our spiritual body needs to eat spiritual food so that we can produce good fruit. God says that man should not live on bread alone for the physical body, but from every word that He as the Creator gives us. If we are to produce fruit, we need to be branches connected to a good vine. In the book of John, Jesus talked about His purpose and his true identity. He said, "I am the true vine, and My Father is the vinedresser. Every branch in me that does not bear fruit He takes away; and every branch that bears fruit, He prunes, that it may bear more fruit."[118]

Notice that He says that in order for us to bear more fruit (or have a purposeful life), we need pruning. Most of us, if we are honest, don't like this idea. We don't want to go through trials or be tested. We want God to be gracious toward us. We don't realize that pruning is actually evidence of God's grace. If the vinedresser does not take notice of our need for pruning, we will be destroyed. Rose bushes that produce the prettiest roses are those that are pruned. A form of grace is the Vinedresser pruning us or, in simpler words, God engaging us. Jesus explained that in order for us to bear fruit we must abide in Him. In order to truly abide in Christ, we must remove sin and other things that can separate us from God. He is the true vine, and if we abide (rest, dwell) in Him then we are able to produce good fruit. But if we do not rest in Him, God says we can do nothing! "I am the true vine, you are the branches. He who abides in me, and I in him, bears much fruit; for without Me you can do nothing."[119] That is a very sobering thought. Pause and let that sink in for a moment. If we are successful on our jobs, and success is measured by what we earn and how others value us, we have done nothing if we don't abide in the Vine. If our marriage is the model one for our family and friends and others express a desire to be more like us, we have done nothing if we don't abide in the Vine. If we write books, songs, poems, or create music and art, we have done nothing if we don't abide in the Vine. This thought will cut to your very soul when you understand it. Jesus is saying that we can do nothing if we are not connected to Him. But, when we abide in Him, these things become meaningful and fruitful, and they can have a profound effect on our life and the lives of others. To live purposefully, we need to be totally dependent upon Him.

For those of us who are parents and have experienced a newborn, we can identify with this type of dependency. The life of a newborn depends on our life.

That infant looks to us for food, water, shelter, clothing, and for us to pick him or her up after every fall. When an infant cries, we comfort them; and when ill, we nurse them back to health. God sees us the exact same way as we see newborns. Newborns are physically unable to function without our help. We offer our constant assistance because we understand that this new creation is undeveloped and needs continual attention. Similarly, God understands that we are unable to function without His constant nurturing and help. Babies ask for help by crying out, but many of us refuse to cry out to God for help. We must exercise the wisdom of newborn babies and cry out to God for wisdom, guidance, and purpose so we can fulfill our destiny!

Newborns eventually become toddlers, and everything around them becomes a possible danger. The things we use for daily living and sustenance, such as an electric socket, can harm a toddler. God our Father sees us the same way. Water and fire are necessary for our daily living, but too much can destroy us. Just as toddlers put their trust in their parents for protection, so are we to put our trust in God our Father. God is there to take care of us, to provide, to comfort, to encourage, to teach, and to instruct. His word sustains us, and He feeds us the milk of His word, as Paul says, until we are able to eat meat. The instructions for life given by the Creator are the food we need to survive. His word is the authority of life, and it is important for us to live in purpose and to bear fruits of purpose, so that we can fulfill our destiny in Him. Destiny can only be fulfilled through purpose. The psalmist says, "Your decrees have been the theme of my songs wherever I have lived. I reflect at night on who you are, O Lord, therefore I obey your instructions."[120]

Some of America's past presidents understood the value of God's word. John Adams, sixth president of the United States, is credited with saying, "In what light soever we regard the Bible, whether with reference to revelation, to history, or to morality, it is an invaluable and inexhaustible mine of knowledge and virtue."[121] Theodore Roosevelt, twenty-sixth US president, is credited with saying, "A thorough knowledge of the Bible is worth more than a college education."[122] A quote attributed to Andrew Jackson, America's seventh president, is, "We who are frequently visited by this chastening rod, have the consolation to read in the Scriptures that whomever He chasteneth He loveth, and does it for their good to make them mindful of their mortality and that this earth is not our abiding place; and afflicts us that we may prepare for a better world, a happy immortality."[123] The sixteenth president of the United States, Abraham Lincoln has been quoted thus: "In regard to this great book, I have but to say, I believe the Bible is the best gift God has given to man. All the good the Savior gave to the world was communicated through this book. But for this book we could not know right from wrong. All things most desirable for man's welfare, here and hereafter, are found portrayed in it."[124] And, finally, Herbert Hoover, thirty-first US president, is credited with stating it this way: "The whole inspiration of our civilization springs from the teachings of Christ and the lessons of the prophets. To read the Bible for these fundamentals is a necessity of American life."[125]

Today, we are consumed with such cares of the world as losing weight, watching what we eat, and dieting. Sometimes our weight gain can be attributed to eating the wrong types of foods or eating artificial foods. But if we eat the right proportions of "real" food, we will be fine. Real food is food that will rot at some point, not the artificially engineered stuff that is manufactured with calories, preservatives, and a number of other scientific substances in it. This is not real food but counterfeit. Jesus says the same thing about the food (substance) we consume. The food that He wants us to eat is real food so that we can produce real fruit. He wants us to eat His word, not the artificial stuff of the world. John spoke of the word this way: "I took the little scroll from the angel's hand and ate it. It tasted sweet as honey in my mouth, but when I had eaten it, my stomach turned sour."[126]

The word of the Creator will get inside you and stir up your purpose. Our purpose can only be fulfilled when we abide in the Vine and in the word of God. An iron cannot be useful if it is not connected to a power source. You can press the iron against the clothes as hard as you can to remove the wrinkles, but they will not be smoothed out without the heat that the power produces. The iron is just a vessel for transmitting the heat and power from the power source; it becomes an agent for power once it is connected. God is the source of our power, and the wrinkles of life—sickness, hurts, fears, hang-ups, doubts, and bad fruit—cannot be smoothed out if we are not connected to the Source. The heat or potency in the iron of your purpose needs the Source to give it life-sustaining power.

God created man and gave him the gift of life and the gift of purpose: "Let us make mankind in our image, in our likeness, so that they may rule over the fish in the sea and the birds in the sky, over the livestock, and over all the creatures that move along the ground. So God created mankind in his own image, in the image of God he created him; male and female he created them."[127] God created man and the land that produces vegetation and the various trees bearing fruit with seed in it. Notice that each fruit contains seeds so that the fruit, once consumed, allows the seed to reproduce itself. It is important to note that the seed has a purpose to grow, but it must be planted, watered, and nurtured. Just as a seed planted and watered can bring forth mangoes, strawberries, and all the other wonderful fruit that we enjoy, so can the seeds of the Spirit. Whatever seed you plant will reap fruit. If you plant the seed of forgiveness, you will reap the tree of reconciliation. If you plant the seed of honesty and integrity, you will reap the tree of trust. If you plant the seed of humility, you will reap the tree of greatness. Likewise, if you plant the seed of sin, you will reap the tree of death. "Do not be deceived, God is not mocked, for whatever a man sows, that he will also reap. For he who sows to his flesh will of the flesh reap corruption, but he who sows to the Spirit will of the Spirit reap everlasting life."[128]

To everything that God created He gave a part of Himself, namely the ability to recreate or multiply. In fact, the very first command He gave to man after He created him was to be fruitful and multiply. God blessed them and said to them, "Be fruitful and multiply; fill the earth and subdue it. Rule over the fish of the sea and the birds of the air and over every living creature that moves on the ground."[129] This command is essential to our operating within our purpose. First, you must understand that you rule over the earth and everything in it. It is a kingdom mindset, similar to what God had when He created you. He did not tell the plants or the fish or the livestock to rule; He gave that purpose to man because He knew man would need that original function in order to fulfill his purpose on earth.

A person who consumes too much alcohol may become dependent and addicted to it. By definition, alcoholism states that a person has lost control. In fact, some may suggest that the alcohol has control over one's life, or rules one's life. This is a direct contradiction to what God states as a purpose for mankind. So we see that whatever man does contrary to what God commands, he loses control of his life, and some other form of creation takes dominion over him (such as alcohol, tobacco, or money). The command was for man to have dominion over creation, not for creation to have dominion over man.

The dominion promise was the first promise of entrepreneurialism. In this promise, the entrepreneurial spirit was born. As basic as food and water, this promise is made to equip us with the tools to be innovative, strategic, and managerial. This is the promise by which I try to govern my life, and as I study successful leaders, they, too, understand this basic principle. In this promise lies the secret to knowing one's ability to become successful through the knowledge of whatever your vision creates. In the garden, God commanded Adam to be fruitful, multiply, and have dominion over the earth. The act of multiplying is the physical sense and one that most of us have taken advantage of. We have been able to multiply through childbirth, but we have not taken full advantage of the promise for faith, wisdom, and purpose—the multiplication of the spiritual qualities of the Creator. Multiplication is much more powerful than addition. It brings great abundance more quickly. What we were not able to do is have dominion over our lives or even over the multiplicity in other areas in our lives. As we multiply, we should subdue. This suggests that God wants us to have abundance, live in abundance, but to exercise control over it, understanding that we are just trustees of his creation. The earth is where we are born, live our lives, and die. It is where we build our homes, our lives, and our families. It is here that we define ourselves, discover purpose, and fulfill our destiny. This is the most basic promise given about the earth, other than the correlation between the earth and the Kingdom. Once we understand this promise and the knowledge of the correlation, we will be able to create in the same mindset of the ultimate Creator. For out of nothing, He created everything, and we have the ability to create anything out of nothing.

One of the most dynamic creations of all time is the Internet. It follows the creation of the telephone and television, which were created out of our need to orate, hear, and visualize things more. Look at other creations—the automobile, airplane, computer, iPod … the list goes on and on. What gave these visionaries and entrepreneurs the bold belief that these things could be created? It was the dominion promise. Adam understood it, and so did many other historical and biblical personalities. Joshua understood it as well. He took the promise to have dominion over the Promised Land.[130] Bill Gates understood it, had dominion of the computer software world, and created a global computer giant. Ray Kroc understood it, had dominion over beef, and grew McDonald's into a global fast food company. Steve Jobs understood it and grew Apple into a global technology leader. The list is nearly endless of people created by God who recreated based on the dominion promise given at the beginning of their existence. They discovered the purpose of their lives and became fruitful and multiplied. The same gift was given to you and I.

God's plan and purpose is to bless you. He gave you the earth and everything good in it so that you would prosper and use it as a blessing. He wants you to produce good fruit so that you can supply the world with sustenance that all might live. Jesus' fruit of His purpose was His word. He spoke the words of God that brought not only healing, deliverance, and abundance, but also wisdom, knowledge, and the fear of God. "For I know the plans I have for you," declares the Lord, "plans to prosper you and not to harm you, plans to give you hope and a future."[131] Your Creator wants to reveal to you His wonderful purpose for your life so that you can produce fruit, with seed, that will continue to produce and be a blessing. All He requires of you is to diligently seek a relationship with Him, keep His commandments, and get into a position so that He can give you your purpose along with all the provisions and blessings you will need.

I love to watch football with my son, Zion, who believes that he will one day be a great wide receiver, tight end, and running back all wrapped up into one awesome player. It probably feeds his ego and desire when he constantly beats me when we play his electronic Madden football game. I enjoy watching games with my family, even though they may not understand the plays; they only care about the touchdowns, the victory. I explain to them that although defense is extremely important, the team that calls the plays the best is usually the one that wins the game. One play that I have pointed out to my family is the timing pass. The timing pass is set up by the quarterback and receiver. The play happens when the receiver runs a route to not necessarily elude the blocker, but rather to get to a spot on the field before the ball gets there. There is an element of trust that has to be present for the play to work. The receiver must trust that the ball will be there, and the quarterback must trust that the receiver will be at the spot—not before he throws the ball, but while the ball is still in the air. The timing pass is one of trust.

God treats us similarly when blessing us. Similar to a quarterback controlling the ball, God is the one who controls our blessings, purpose, desires, finances, families—our very lives. We need to trust Him in every area. The ball might represent health, wealth, happiness, money, marriage, relationship, or some other need or desire we have. As the quarterback throws the ball before the receiver gets there, God may throw a blessing our way and tell us what we need to do to run to the right spot to receive it. He has told us to keep His commandments and to love the Lord our God with all our heart, with all our soul, and with all our mind.[132]

Many of us, not knowing that our blessing is on the way, refuse to run the route, and refuse to follow God's word. The book of Proverbs says, "Many are the plans in a man's heart, but it is the Lord's purpose that prevails."[133] God has the purpose for us, and all we need to do is ask Him for it and trust Him. When the receiver is running a play, he believes that he is running in order to meet the ball at its intended end place, but after he catches the ball, he has to run another route and avoid the defenders to get the victory. So the timing play route acts as training for him before the ball arrives because he will have to contend with more forces trying to stop him from getting his victory once he receives the ball. There may be only one or two defenders dedicated to stopping him at first, but once he has the ball, the entire defensive team will pursue him.

Doesn't that sound like life? People with a negative mindset will try to block you from receiving your blessings and from fulfilling your purpose. But you first have to trust God and run His route to receive the training for your blessing's arrival. Your battle does not end when you discover your purpose; it's just beginning. You will need those same skills to carry your purpose and blessing on to destiny. Once you catch the blessing from God, He then helps to protect it from those trying to stop you. He protects your blind side and is your lead blocker on the field of life. God promises, "Vengeance is mine; and recompense; their foot shall slip in due time; for the day of the calamity is at hand, and the things to come hasten upon them."[134]

The enemy is more armed once your knowledge of purpose is revealed. He calls in the other teammates to stop you from reaching your goal, but God says, "You, dear children, are from God and have overcome them, because the one who is in you is greater than the one who is in the world."[135] In other words, you possess the most powerful force in the world: God Himself.

We are being prepared before we catch His blessings. Our beliefs, thoughts, attitudes, speech, actions, and character are all a part of our training. Notice that the foundation is our thoughts and beliefs, because we build our attitude, speech, actions, and character from our thoughts and beliefs. That is the foundation of who we are. We may need to reposition ourselves in order to receive our purpose and our blessing, like the receiver had to be in a different position to receive the ball. First, we must reposition our minds and our hearts and trust God, our Creator, to ensure that we get the victory and produce the fruits of our purpose.

God "threw" Joseph's purpose and blessing toward Egypt, and when Joseph was repositioned, he was able to operate in his purpose. Often God needs to reposition us in order for us to receive our blessings and operate in His purpose for our lives. Joseph was to be governor and save the Israelites from famine, including his brothers, father, and family. Joseph endured hardships, trials, ridicule, and persecution at the hands of his family. But he ran his route through slavery, through servanthood, through prison, and finally to the palace where his purpose would be revealed and he would be victorious. Joseph understood that in order to get *to*, you must go *through*! Whatever people do to you, God will turn it around; be ready to run your route and position yourself in God to receive your purpose and prosperity for your life.

The fruits of purpose will take on the things that money cannot buy. Many of us believe that the fruits of purpose are financial and physical, and in some cases this is true. But God also wants your fruits to be more than finite; He's aiming for everlasting. He says, "The fruit of the Spirit is love, joy, peace, patience, kindness, goodness, faithfulness, gentleness and self-control."[136] These fruits are a strong tower with love as the foundation. God is love and gave His son because He so loved the world. Without love, the other fruits would be meaningless. Love is the foundation and cornerstone that allows joy to be built upon. Joy, unlike happiness, does not come from what happens to us externally, but from what we know within. Once we have love and joy, we can experience peace, patience, goodness, faithfulness, gentleness, and finally self-control. If we look at each of these fruits, we can discover something about our purpose. The fruits of purpose and the fruit of the Spirit can speak to the purpose of our lives.

For example, if we genuinely love to see young people learn and are zealous about wiping out illiteracy, our true purpose may lie in educating our youth. If we can demonstrate patience in teaching young people and be faithful in our commitment to them, this additionally may point toward a purpose as a teacher. Teaching is a very noble profession and must be celebrated, as the youth are our future, and we must ensure that they are able to advance. Moreover, it is our responsibility to ensure that we teach them about their Creator and that everything that exists was and is in Him.

People spend their entire lives trying to find love and peace. They look to the wrong person for love and find heartache and devastation. They look to find joy or happiness in work and careers, but find themselves unhappy and unfulfilled. God wants you to look to His Spirit for those things that money and people can't give you. If we possessed such fruits, we would be able to fulfill our purpose in the way God intended. The fruits of our purpose would be a reward to mankind and us. We could make a difference in the lives of people and touch future generations.

Now if the fruit of the Spirit is love, joy, peace, patience, goodness, kindness, gentleness, faithfulness, and self-control, one can deduce that the fruits of the flesh are hate, sorrow, war, impatience, evil, cruelty, abrasiveness, unfaithfulness, and unruliness. Christ said that we will know people by their fruits (actions or traits). Paul said that the flesh wars against the Spirit. The things he knows that he should do, he doesn't, and the things he knows he shouldn't do, he does. The word of God also says we (in the flesh) should prosper even as our soul (in the spirit) prospers. Anyone not living according to the fruits of the Spirit is living according to the fruits of the flesh, so do not be surprised if they demonstrate one or all of these fruits of the flesh.

In order to fulfill our purpose, we need to live according to the Spirit of God, or we will fulfill a purpose according to the flesh of man. God says if a person be found faithful, He will show up. He does not require us to be successful, wealthy, or beautiful, but to be faithful. Study and read His word. Keep His word. Be faithful. Revelation 2:10 says for you to remain faithful until death and God will give you the crown of life. Don't quit on God or yourself! Follow after the fruits of the spirit. If everyone else bows, turn away, do not follow man, but follow God. Stay faithful to God, and He will establish your purpose and bless you!

Jesus was aware of the fruits of the flesh. That is why He warned about false prophets. Their words are many, but the fruit of their lives is self-evident. In the book of Matthew, Jesus told His disciples, "Watch out for false prophets. They come to you in sheep's clothing, but inwardly they are ferocious wolves. By their fruit you will recognize them. Do people pick grapes from thorn bushes, or figs from thistles? Likewise every good tree bears good fruit, but a bad tree bears bad fruit. A good tree cannot bear bad fruit, and a bad tree cannot bear good fruit."[137] We see the connection of man and his seed to fruit of a tree and its seed or fruit. Your purpose will produce good fruit that everyone will recognize, making a difference in the world according to your fruits of purpose.

Chapter Eight
It Will Prevail

❧

"The Lord Almighty has sworn, Surely, as I have planned, so it will be, and as I have purposed, so it will stand."

ISAIAH 14:24

"So is my word that goes out from my mouth: It will not return to me empty, but will accomplish what I desire and achieve the purpose for which I sent it."

ISAIAH 55:11

"Purpose drives your life and destiny. The purpose of God will define your life, but the plans of man without God, will confine it."

RICARDO A. RICHARDSON

There have been many people born in less than desirable circumstances, but their purpose in life has prevailed. There is a storied list of individuals who were orphans and later achieved success in life. Raised in orphanages or homes absent of their parents did not cancel the assignment of purpose for their lives. Among such were Aristotle, an influential philosopher in the history of Western thought; Johann Sebastian Bach, the famous organist and music composer; George Washington Carver, educator, chemist, and one of the world's greatest inventors; Nelson Rolihlahla Mandela, the first democratically elected president of South Africa; Steven Paul Jobs, the founder and CEO of Apple Inc; Andrew Jackson, seventh president of the United States; and William Jefferson Clinton, forty-second president of the United States. These people led their respective fields and professions despite growing up as orphans or foster children. Every life is valuable and has purpose. The gift of purpose for these lives pursued them until it was realized. No matter their beginnings, obstacles, or circumstances along the way, each understood that their life had purpose, and they were able to draw out that purpose and prevail.

By now you have wrapped your mind around the concept that purpose is a gift buried deep within you, at the core, waiting to be revealed, and once you get into God's word and will, your purpose will be revealed and actively pursue you. Your Creator is the one who gave you your parents, your life, and your purpose. I want you to realize that purpose will prevail; it must, regardless if you accept it or not. The one who accepts and receives purpose will operate in it; the one who does not accept his purpose will be operated by it nonetheless.

Joseph understood his purpose for living, but his brothers did not. Joseph's purpose governed his life, and he operated in it, but his brothers were agents of the purpose and were operated by it. This was born out in their plan to destroy Joseph's purpose, but Joseph's purpose used their plan to promote it. Many people, like Joseph's brothers, are so busy focusing on how to destroy the purpose of others that they miss out on what their true purpose was intended to be. Instead of using their purposes, they are used by others' purposes. Simply stated, they become *agents* of purpose or people who operate in their *own* purpose, not in God's purpose for them.

When Esther found out from Mordecai that the Jews were going to be annihilated, she hesitated in going to King Xerxes for fear of her life. Mordecai reminded her that if she did not go, she, too, would be put to death because she was a Jew. It seems as though Esther had forgotten who she was at the core since becoming queen. Mordecai reminded her that she had been made queen for such a time as this: to save her people. In essence, Esther accepted her assignment of purpose and became an agent for that purpose. If she had rejected it, she would have forfeited the protection that her purpose would have afforded her through God and most likely exposed herself to probable death because of her Jewish heritage.

Purpose will prevail in your life or, if rejected, in the life of another. It is your choice to serve as an agent of purpose or an agent of somebody else's purpose. Proverbs says, "Death and life are in the power of the tongue, and those who love it will eat its fruit."[138] This means that you have the choice to accept the purpose God has for your life, to speak His words, and to live by them. By accepting the assignment of purpose, you will then eat of the good fruits of purpose and live a productive, fruitful life. You can only accept the assignment by connecting to the Creator, the revealer of all purposes and mysteries of life.

A good example of this is Gideon. God had a purpose for him, but at first Gideon could not accept that purpose because he thought less of himself. He eventually accepted the purpose, after it relentlessly pursued him, and he became an agent of purpose and a mighty warrior. As background, throughout the book of Judges, the Israelites would look to a judge to save them from the result of their turning from God after forty years of peace brought by Deborah's victory over Canaan. Deborah was a prophetess of God and a judge of Israel. After the Israelites rebelled against God, the Midianites enslaved them for seven years. In captivity, the Israelites bowed down to the idols of their oppressors, so God chose Gideon to deliver His people. Gideon was threshing wheat in a winepress, hiding from the Midianites, because whenever the Israelites planted crops, the enemy would invade the towns and take their property. So there was Gideon, hiding from the enemy. The angel of the Lord appeared to Gideon while he was hiding and called him a mighty warrior.

The angel of the Lord came and sat down under the oak in Ophrah that belonged to Joash the Abiezrite, where his son Gideon was threshing wheat in a winepress to keep it from the Midianites. When the angel of the Lord appeared to Gideon, he said, "The Lord is with you, mighty warrior." "But sir," Gideon replied, "if the Lord is with us, why has all this happened to us? Where are all his wonders that our fathers told us about when they said, 'Did not the Lord bring us up out of Egypt?' But now the Lord has abandoned us and put us into the hand of Midian." The Lord turned to him and said, "Go in the strength you have and save Israel out of Midian's hand. Am I not sending you?" "But Lord," Gideon asked, "how can I save Israel? My clan is the weakest in Manasseh, and I am the least in my family." The Lord answered, "I will be with you, and you will strike down all the Midianites together." Gideon replied, "If now I have found favor in your eyes, give me a sign that it is really you talking to me. Please do not go away until I come back and bring my offering and set it before you." And the Lord said, "I will wait until your return."[139]

Can you picture the scene? Gideon is hiding in the winepress, hurrying to thresh the wheat before the enemy comes, and the Lord appears to him and calls him a mighty warrior. This is a great illustration of purpose revealed. Even though Gideon was hiding and acting cowardly, his purpose still identified and defined him. Gideon's cowardliness was being redefined by his purpose as a mighty warrior. As long as we continually acknowledge and seek God, He will reveal our purpose to us, in some cases, quite unexpectedly.

Gideon's response to being called a mighty warrior was, "Who, me?" Don't we often do the same when God calls us to the purpose He has for us? Like many of us, Gideon made excuse after excuse to avoid his purpose. He had convinced himself that he and his people would be defeated because God had abandoned them. He looked to everything and everyone else but himself. When the angel replied for Gideon to "go in the strength you have and save Israel,"[140] I am surprised Gideon did not faint! Gideon's answer of being the weakest clan and the weakest member shows he was focusing and relying on himself, not on God. But God ignored Gideon's background and lack of courage and promised that He would be with him and together they would strike down the Midianites. God was not focusing on Gideon's history or his heritage, but on His own strength.

This has been my point all along. You must seek God so that He will be with you, then you are guaranteed success in whatever He purposes you to do. It is God's strength that is made perfect in our weaknesses. The apostle Paul realized this when he asked God to remove a thorn in his side and God said no: "My grace is sufficient for you, for my power is made perfect in weakness. Therefore I will boast all the more gladly about my weaknesses, so that Christ's power may rest on me. That is why, for Christ's sake, I delight in weaknesses, in insults, in hardships, in persecutions, in difficulties. For when I am weak, then I am strong."[141]

Gideon was like most of us: He doubted what God said and wanted proof. How many times have we asked God to show us a sign or two, only to believe God and then doubt again? You need to practice what God says to you so that you can become skilled in the commands of God and know beyond the shadow of a doubt that you are able to conceive, deliver, and execute your purpose.

As the story continues, God gave Gideon his orders to fight against the Midianites, but before that, He tested Gideon's beliefs in his own bravery. God used obedience in Gideon's life as a training ground for his purpose. He instructed Gideon to tear down his father's altar to pagan god Baal and cut down the Asherah pole, a symbol of devotion to the like-named goddess. Then he instructed Gideon on the proper kind of altar—one to honor the Lord God—to erect. Gideon followed God's commands, but because he was afraid, he erected it at night rather than in the daytime. As he suspected, the men of the town were furious and demanded Gideon's life, but his father, Joash, pleaded his case. After this test of obedience,

Gideon said to God, "If you will save Israel by my hand as you have prom-ised—look, I will place a wool fleece on the threshing floor. If there is dew only on the fleece and all the ground is dry, then I will know that you will save Israel by my hand, as you said.' And that is what happened. Gideon rose early the next day; he squeezed the fleece and wrung out the dew—a bowlful of water. Then Gideon said to God, "Do not be angry with me. Let me make just one more request. Allow me one more test with the fleece, but this time make the fleece dry and let the ground be covered with dew." That night God did so. Only the fleece was dry; all the ground was covered with dew.[142]

This doubt by Gideon and reaffirmation by God could have continued on and on. Sometimes we ask God for one sign, then another, and another, and don't realize how much time has passed because of our doubts. We then wonder what has happened to the promise and why God has not blessed us. It is our doubt that prolongs our anxiety and delays our victory!

Gideon doubted that he had courage and could do as the Lord instructed him. He was very unsure of both God's commands and himself and requested God to show him proof by performing exact opposite miracles. This says that Gideon wanted not only proof that he would be able to save the Israelites, but proof that God's power is really as He says it is. Gideon then sent out messengers to gather all the men from the tribes of Asher, Zebulun, Naphtali, as well as his own tribe, Manasseh. He wanted as much help as he could get to fight the enemy because he still doubted. But God told him to cut the number amassed because He wanted no doubt about the deliverance of the people. His purpose was for them to be delivered by the hand of Gideon but to *His* glory, so that the people would realize that it was not done in their own strength.

God instructed Gideon to send home the men who were afraid, and 22,000 men left, leaving behind 10,000, which was still too many according to God. The Lord told Gideon to take the men down to the water. God said, "If I say, 'This one shall go with you,' he shall go; but if I say, 'This one shall not go with you,' he shall not go."[143] So Gideon took the men down to the water. There the Lord told him to separate those who lapped the water with their tongues like a dog from those who knelt down to drink. Three hundred men lapped with their hands to their mouths. All the rest got down on their knees to drink. The Lord said to Gideon, "With the three hundred men that lapped I will save you and give the Midianites into your hands. Let the others go home."[144] So Gideon sent the rest of the Israelites to their tents, but kept the three hundred who then took over the provisions and trumpets of the others.

God is saying that he only wanted the men who lapped like dogs to follow Gideon so that there would be no doubt who would get the glory for the victory. Dogs are loyal followers and obey every command of their master. When our master and Creator gives us instructions, we often try to reason and rationalize those instructions. That is why God requested that Gideon only recruit the ones who could take instruction. Gideon would have probably been numbered among the three hundred if he had been recruited for the Israelite army, because he knew how to take instructions. I wonder, if God had assembled other mighty men to help Gideon, would they have been able to take orders from him? I don't think they would have respected Gideon's words as being their Savior's words. They knew Gideon's reputation as a coward and would probably not have fought under his command. God has to decrease us in order to increase Himself, because often we believe that we have the answer and our way is the only way, the right way. Proverbs says, "There is a way that seems right to a man, but in the end it leads to death."[145] God always knew He would be the one fighting against the Midianites, and Gideon's purpose was connected to God. Whenever God gives a promise of purpose, He has to fulfill that promise, not for your sake, but for His own.

The Bible says, "God is not a man that he should tell a lie, neither a human being, that he should change his mind. Does He speak and then not act? Does He promise and not fulfill?"[146] He wanted to prove to Gideon and all of the Israelites that He alone is sovereign and uses the individual purpose of men to fulfill His ultimate, universal purpose. He used the weakest man of the weakest family, of the weakest clan of the Israelites, and He can use you and me to fulfill our purposes regardless of what others think of us or what we think of ourselves.

God realizes our weaknesses, faults, and shortcomings as He did with Gideon, knowing that he was still growing in his courage and purpose. So God sent him during the night to the Midian camp to listen to what they were saying. Gideon overheard a Midianite talking about his dream of how their camp was destroyed. Another soldier responded that this could only be the sword of Gideon, and that God had given the Midianites and the whole camp into Gideon's hands. When Gideon heard the dream and interpretation, he worshipped God for His encouragement. God gave Gideon confirmation because he knew that he still doubted his courage and the power of God. God's encouragement gave Gideon boldness. He returned to the camp and divided the three hundred men into three companies, giving each trumpets and torches. Overnight, Gideon turned into a mighty warrior, walking in his purpose:

> *"Watch me," he told them. "Follow my lead. When I get to the edge of the camp, do exactly as I do. When I and all who are with me blow our trumpets, then from all around the camp blow yours and shout, 'For the Lord and for Gideon.'"* *Gideon and the hundred men with him reached the edge of the camp at the beginning of the middle watch, just after they had changed the guard. They blew their trumpets and broke the jars that were in their hands. The three companies blew the trumpets and smashed the jars. Grasping the torches in their left hands and holding in their right hands the trumpets they were to blow, they shouted, "A sword for the Lord and for Gideon!" While each man held his position around the camp, all the Midianites ran, crying out as they fled. When the three hundred trumpets sounded, the Lord caused the men throughout the camp to turn on each other with their swords. The army fled to Beth Shittah toward Zererah as far as the border of Abel Meholah near Tabbath.*[147]

How bold Gideon became! "Watch me!" he declared. "Follow my lead!" "For the Lord and for Gideon!" He knew to put God first! Who was this new person? He was not a weakling, surely not a coward. This sounds like a warrior! These are the words of a leader and commander. Gideon was transformed from a coward into a mighty warrior. The key ingredient in his transformation was his belief in what God called him, his true identity: mighty warrior. Gideon didn't go to the Israelite school of military training or another leadership school for training, yet he was operating in the purpose to which God called him.

At the end of the story, the Midianites ran away, afraid for their lives. Gideon, honoring God, sent out the men from the Ephraim clan to pursue them, while he and 300 men pursued the two Midianite kings. After Gideon returned, the Israelites pleaded with him to be their leader and king, but he refused. Gideon honored God because he realized what the Israelites originally thought about him and who he was based on what God had told him. Gideon informed them that God would be their ruler.

God demonstrated patience in helping Gideon see himself as God saw him.

He encouraged him and nurtured him until he became a mighty warrior. God demonstrated to Gideon that his purpose would prevail in spite of his fear and doubt. All the men in his village, including his family, considered him a failure. This resulted in Gideon having low self-esteem. But God first gave him instructions to see if he would obey. Obedience is important to understanding what the Creator wants for us. Once we understand who we are and exercise obedience, our faith will increase and so will our courage to face our fears. After believing God, Gideon was able to believe in himself, and his bravery grew. God said that he was more than what others thought about him and would be the only person among the Israelites to save them. God is saying to you as well that you have a purpose that will make you mighty and potent. Your worth is in Him, so you must disregard what anyone else thinks of you. Lift your head high and act boldly as Gideon did because you are mighty in God's eyes.

Coach James "Jim" Ellis formed the first African-American swim team at the Marcus Foster Recreation Center in Philadelphia, Pennsylvania. The team, formed in 1971, was named the PDR swim team. Although the letters stood for the Philadelphia Department of Recreation, he instilled pride, determination, and resilience into these troubled youths. He made his students focus on what's inside, not on the outside appearance of the recreation center or themselves. The center looked dilapidated on the outside, but the indoor pool was in good condition and functional. Similarly, the swim team had been judged by their outward appearance, but what was on the inside is what mattered and is what, ultimately, gave them victory. The swimmers focused on their coach and what PDR stood for to them. It wasn't about what they looked like, where they came from, or how others saw them; it was about what they knew internally about themselves. They focused not on their reputation but on their identity of purpose.

No one on the outside could see the swimmers' purpose or resolve, but it prevailed as Coach Ellis encountered opposition in keeping the recreation center opened and competing against experienced swim teams. After thirty-seven years, he still coaches swimming at the Marcus Foster pool and has sent swimmers to the Olympic trials for every US team since 1992.[148] His protégés include Michael Norment, the first black swimmer on the US national team.

In 2007, Ellis received the President's Award from the International Swimming Hall of Fame. Coach Ellis' purpose to mentor and coach his swim team took them into unchartered waters, no pun intended. Swimming is not a sport often practiced in the African-American community, but Ellis' purpose prevailed against all odds. The purpose of this group of determined and dedicated individuals broke barriers and opened doors that had been locked for years. Hollywood later made a movie titled *Pride* about Ellis' life and the experiences of the young swimmers he mentored. My family enjoys this true inspirational story about how purpose can prevail under any circumstance.

Your purpose, too, can prevail in unchartered waters. In fact, God will not call you to do something you have already done before. Your purpose will take you to uncharted waters, but the good news is that God will captain your vessel and guide you to your destiny through your purpose. He wants to show you that nothing is impossible with Him, and what seems impossible or unlikely is in His favor.

When we focus on the right thing, everything else becomes insignificant. Many of us heard about the story of Daniel in the lions' den and how God shut the mouths of the lions. If we were to look at this story pictorially, we may notice that Daniel focused on the Lord and not the lions. Focusing on God makes all of our problems seem smaller and their roars much more like a kitten's meow.

The purpose to write this book has been pursuing me all my life. But I must admit that I had very different plans that did not prevail. "Many are the plans in a person's heart, but it is the Lord's purpose that prevails."[149] I have to be honest and say that I never thought I would author a book. I still don't think of myself as an author, and I give God all the glory for the manifestation of this book. I responded as Gideon did and then had doubts that I would be able to write it. I made excuse after excuse, but God's purpose still pursued me, and He patiently waited on me. I tried to bargain with God, claiming to be busy with other things for the kingdom and to help people. I reminded Him that I have always tried to serve others. But God knew what He wanted of me, and that purpose would prevail in my life because I love Him and pursue Him. Serving is always a part of the purpose that God has called us to, but for now, my unique purpose is to write this book.

I am writing this from personal experiences, from a place of discomfort. It is in this place that God can pour into me in order to pour into this book. I was frustrated for a very long time until I accepted God's purpose for my life. I have made excuses in my life of not being adequate or qualified. I wanted everything to be perfect. I wanted to live in the right house, in the right neighborhood, and have the right family. I would say as Gideon did that I am not useful and cannot impact the world like others can. How can I possibly write a book about purpose? How can I write any book, for that matter? The truth is, I still feel that way. I am still planning things in my life with family and service in which I can make a difference, but now I do it as a service unto the Lord. I find contentment in it, and ask God to show me His purpose in everything I do.

I am a work in progress, like Gideon, and need encouragement from God daily. But He understands that I need Him to be patient with me and to encourage me during times of trouble and doubt. I am writing this book to encourage you that if I can petition the Creator to give me the knowledge and understanding to get through the slices of life and go deep to the core—draw out the deep purposes that exist in my heart—so can you. You may not know what your plans are, but your Creator says that His plans are to prosper you and not to harm you, to give you a life of hope and of purpose.[150]

Chapter Nine

Living on Purpose

⟷

"Those who cleanse themselves from the latter will be instruments for noble purposes, made holy, useful to the Master and prepared to do any good work."

2 TIMOTHY 2:21 NIV

"God gives purpose as He gives life, and purpose gives life the velocity that will drive you to your destiny."

RICARDO A. RICHARDSON

H ave you ever noticed that people who know their purpose in life seem driven and passionate? What gets them going in the morning? Why are they so driven, lively, and inspired? Why do they give it their best? They are living their lives on purpose and for purpose. The fact that you are alive today means there is a purpose for you being here. You must allow God to manifest His purpose for you to live for. The purpose of life is to live it, and a life of purpose is worth both living and dying for. Those driven by this believe in what they are called to do so much that they would die for it. In fact, that is what passion is. As a former collegiate athlete and basketball executive, I can easily spot players that have talent. There are a number of athletes that played in the ABA, CBA, or NCAA that have more talent than some of the players in the NBA. But, the difference between the players that make it to the highest level is passion. It drives them to be the best and, more importantly, "give" their best.

Purpose is what breathes passion for you to be driven. Swiss philosopher and poet Henri-Frédéric Amiel once said, "A man without passion is only a latent force, only a possibility, like a stone waiting for a blow from the iron to give forth sparks."[151] We can all relate to this. Passion causes us to press forward even when we don't have the strength to do so. Jesus had purpose and passion. He died for what He believed in. You have to be willing to die to protect and fulfill your purpose. Jesus embodied this. He had a purpose that gave him the passion to die for mankind. He was falsely accused, which led to his death, yet He held onto His passion and purpose. Now, I am sure that you are looking at purpose a little differently. What are you living for? The answer should be that which you would die for. Purpose will give you something to die for, not just live for.

Solomon had a purpose and passion given him from his father, King David, and from God. David received his anointing for his purpose—to be king of Israel—from the prophet Samuel. And with this gift came power and passion. David was passionate about leadership. He protected the sheep as a young shepherd and was willing to die to save their lives. He fought the bear and the lion and overcame them both. Then when Goliath mocked the Israelites, David showed great passion and courage and fought and defeated him. David was willing to give his life for what he believed in. God wants us to be passionate about our purpose, and He will protect our purpose from harm. Solomon not only inherited the crown, he also inherited his father's passion and purpose.

David anointed Solomon, his successor, to sit on the throne in his place, even though his other son, Adonijah, had made himself king. David instructed Solomon to be strong and honor God in everything that he did and to keep God's commands and decrees. If he followed this path, everything he did would be prosperous. David left the kingdom to Solomon in good standing and in peace. He and his attendants set Solomon's reign in motion at a very high level. When Solomon took office, he established his leadership quickly by following his father's commands to bless those who blessed his father, and remove those who cursed him. Solomon had an encounter with God, which would equip him to be the wisest king, enabling him to fulfill his purpose for God:

> *The king went to Gibeon to offer sacrifices, for that was the most important high place, and Solomon offered a thousand burnt offerings on that altar. At Gibeon the Lord appeared to Solomon during the night in a dream, and God said, "Ask for whatever you want me to give you." Solomon answered, "You have shown great kindness to your servant, my father David, because he was faithful to you and righteous and upright in heart. You have continued this great kindness to him and have given him a son to sit on his throne this very day. Now, O Lord my God, you have made your servant king in place of my father David. But I am only a little child and do not know how to carry out my duties. Your servant is here among the people you have chosen, a great people, too numerous to count or number. So give your servant a discerning heart to govern*

*your people and to distinguish between right and wrong. For who is able to
govern this great people of yours?"*

*The Lord was pleased that Solomon had asked for this. So God said to
him, "Since you have asked for this and not for long life or wealth for yourself,
nor have asked for the death of your enemies but for discernment in adminis-
tering justice, I will do what you have asked. I will give you a wise and discerning heart, so that there will never have been anyone like you, nor will there
ever be. Moreover, I will give you what you have not asked for—both riches
and honor—so that in your lifetime you will have no equal among kings. And
if you walk in my ways and obey my statutes and commands as David your
father did, I will give you a long life." Then Solomon awoke—and he realized
it had been a dream.*[152]

Solomon asked his Creator to give him a wise and discerning heart, and that
is just what he got. God gave him wisdom, which was, in fact, essential for
Solomon's purpose. Solomon asked for wisdom because He was already at the
core communing with God. When you are in communion with God, you know
exactly what to ask for, and whether you ask or not, He will give you good gifts.
He gave Solomon that which he asked for and other gifts that he didn't.

By the age of twenty-two, Solomon had selected his government, officials,
and governors; negotiated peace treaties; governed fairly; and cultivated favor
among his people. He was exercising the wisdom that God had given him with
such potency that kings and queens from surrounding nations came to get his
counsel. God gave Solomon wisdom and very great insight, and a breadth of
understanding as measureless as the sand on the seashore. Solomon's wisdom
was greater than the wisdom of all the men of the East, and greater than all the
wisdom of Egypt.[153] He had won the hearts of the people, and everyone in his
kingdom paid him honor and respect. God told him that because he had asked
for the things that matter the most, He would also grant him the things that mattered the least to Him. Solomon knew that God is only motivated by the heart,
and that is what he asked God for: a discerning heart. This single important gift
helped define his reign as king. Of all the things that Solomon did, we remember
him as the wisest king that ever lived.

Solomon could have easily sat back and enjoyed the fruits of his father's work
and his own. God had blessed him with great knowledge and great wealth. But

Solomon's purpose was to build the temple of God so that the people could get back to true worship. Instead of focusing on all his wealth and desires, he focused on his purpose: the Lord's temple. He realized that purpose and passion is the driving force that would allow him to complete the monumental task of constructing the temple. As the wisest man in the land, Solomon knew such a task was beyond his means. But he had the passion to complete his purpose with such precision that he built the most beautiful temple anyone in the land had ever seen. He gave God nothing short of his best. Solomon built the temple with such excellence that God approved by telling him, "I have heard the prayer you have made before me; I have consecrated this temple, which you have built, by putting my Name there forever. My eyes and my heart will always be there."[154]

God gave his approval because Solomon had put forth his best. He embraced his purpose with passion and continued steadfastly until God's house was completed. God's house was symbolic of his continual dwelling with the people. Solomon took every detail into account and spared no expense in completing a magnificent house for God. The priests went into the temple to perform their duties, but the glory of the Lord filled the temple in a dark cloud. God's glory and presence rested there and resided with the people and a king who wanted His presence. This is good news, as it symbolizes God's desire to reside with you. He wants to show you His glory in your daily life.

After he completed the temple, Solomon proudly declared:

"The Lord has said that he would dwell in a dark cloud; I have indeed built a magnificent temple for you, a place for you to dwell forever." While the whole assembly of Israel was standing there, the king turned around and blessed them. Then he said, "Praise be to the Lord, the God of Israel, who with his own hand has fulfilled what he promised with his own mouth to my father David. For he said, 'Since the day I brought my people Israel out of Egypt, I have not chosen a city in any tribe of Israel to have a temple built for my Name to be there, but I have chosen David to rule my people Israel.' My father David had it in his heart to build a temple for the Name of the Lord, the God of Israel. But the Lord said to my father David, 'Because it was in your heart to build a temple for my Name, you did well to have this in your heart. Nevertheless, you are not the one to build the temple, but your son, who is your own flesh and blood— he is the one who will build the temple for my Name.' The Lord has kept the

promise he made: I have succeeded David my father and now I sit on the throne of Israel, just as the Lord promised, and I have built the temple for the Name of the Lord, the God of Israel. I have provided a place there for the ark, in which is the covenant of the Lord that he made with our fathers when he brought them out of Egypt."[155]

Solomon taught us that purpose and passion drive our lives. We live on purpose and live out passion. With all of his faults and the accolades Solomon received, he remained focused on his purpose, constructing a temple worthy of the Lord's name. Solomon was also renowned for his other architectural projects. After he completed the Lord's temple, he spent thirteen years building his own palace, and he also built a city wall, a citadel, and a palace for the daughter of Pharaoh. Solomon was the chief architect of his time. What drives you and ignites your passion? Remember, Solomon paid attention to ask God for what mattered to Him the most, not what mattered to Solomon, asking for wisdom over wealth. Ask God to reveal your purpose, which will ignite your passion to bless others. Living on purpose will give you something you would give your life for. Solomon rose to his purpose with passion, as did his father, David. He rose to the occasion for God.

I believe American author Suzanne Weyn said it best: "Your life is an occasion, rise to it."[156] Many have died without rising to the occasion of their life. You still have a chance to make a difference in your life and the lives of others. Your life experiences to this point are a source of strength to you and others. In fact, because you are reading the pages of this book means you still have an opportunity to operate in your purpose and live a fulfilling life. What you have overcome, someone else is still struggling with. Be an Elizabeth to them, an example of God doing the impossible of what others believe cannot be done. Be an example for them to follow and find the Elizabeth who has risen to the occasion of her life and overcome what you are dealing with.

People often operate in their gifts and use them for fame and monetary gain. But when you realize that your gift is for a purpose, you begin to operate for those things that money can't buy. You begin to invest in people and give of yourself to help others to achieve a better life. Steve Harvey, gifted comedian, actor, entertainer, and now best-selling author, shifted his purpose through the use of the same gift. I grew up watching *The Steve Harvey Show* and viewed his many movie roles and comedic standup routines. He used his gift and purpose to make people laugh and to entertain. But his purpose grew more potent as he started to seek and celebrate God. Many listeners tune into his morning radio show to brighten up their day with laughter, only to hear him pray for guidance from God before his show begins. He unapologetically gives honor and thanks to God for the blessings in his life and encourages listeners to have a committed prayer life. He and his wife founded a foundation to share, teach, and demonstrate the principles of manhood to young men, enabling them to achieve their dreams and become productive men who are balanced emotionally, politically, and economically.[157]

There are so many problems plaguing young men in the inner city and in general. This mentoring program exposes them to positive role models that can have a profound impact on their lives. Steve Harvey used the same comedic gift God gave to him to fulfill a greater purpose that touches the lives of young men and women through his foundation and radio program. He still entertains but does it with a greater sense of purpose. His accolades are no longer just to the kings of comedy, but to the King of kings, the Lord Jesus Christ.

Living a life of purpose was what one of my former business associates had been searching to do all his life. Although he operated a very successful business, he was still constantly searching for a deeper meaning to his life. At age thirty, he became a devotee of Krishna consciousness and remained in that religion for thirty-three years. Prior to his devotion to Krishna, he became a complete atheist, focusing on scientology. He believed more in creation than the Creator, worshiping idols, animals, and other gods made of human hands. He told me that he received mystic books in the mail for free, not knowing their origin, but he depended on them for daily living and guidance. As an atheist, he could argue the philosophical point of view against the existence of God with such persuasion that he usually would silence some Christian believers. His unbelief in a god or a supreme being was replaced when he followed several gods in Hinduism. The transformation started when we journeyed to India, where the Krishna consciousness and Hindu faith is widespread and commonplace. I visited the temples and observed the dedicated worship of the many idols that took place there. They worshipped the cow and other animals, but with so much reference and dedication that he was proud of this religious devotion. It made me think of the Israelites that worshipped idols of silver and gold made with their own hands. The psalmist recorded this in Psalm 115, stating that these "handmade gods" have mouths, but cannot speak; eyes, but cannot see; ears, but cannot hear; noses, but cannot smell; hands, but cannot feel. He goes on to say that those who made them and those who trust in them, even though they did not create them, shall be like them!" In other words, if we put our trust in anything made in creation that is deaf, blind, or dumb, we ultimately become just like that created thing—deaf, blind, and dumb. In essence, when we let blind idols lead us, we end up falling into a pit.

Jesus confirmed this also when He addressed blind men leading other blind men who ultimately end up in a pit. The blindness Jesus refers[158] to is the lack of knowledge of God. What Jesus is saying is that if you put your trust in the blind, you will be blind, so the converse is that if you put your trust in the all-seeing God, then you will be able to see and live. If we do not know who our Creator truly is and put our complete belief and trust in Him, then we are blind. And if we are blind, how can we see our purpose? How can we see what we are supposed to do with our life? How can I know who I am, if I cannot see the I AM?

Sometime later my Hindu associate and I visited the Christian churches and temples in Ethiopia, and he made a comment to me about the worship by the devoted Christians there. He mentioned to me that if the Christians in the Western world had reverence, devotion, and worshipped God in the way that the Christians in Ethiopia did, he would not have converted to the Hindu faith. At that point, I knew that he was still searching, and God was working on his heart. We would have open discussions about my faith in Jesus Christ, and I would never judge him. I continued to pray that God would open up his heart to search for Him and reveal to him the purpose of his life.

I have seen the longing fulfilled in his life for his purpose. He has accepted Jesus Christ as his personal savior and is communicating the truth that he discovered with other devotees of the Krishna, Muslim, and Hindu faiths. Because he has been a student of many religions, he is able to go deeper into himself and search the scriptures to discover who his Creator is and why he was created. He started focusing on the spirituality of Christ as opposed to the religion of man. As a result, God has revealed to him the purpose for his life and he is content to walk in that purpose. God protected his heart, and although his mind was able to get deeper into the various religions of the world, his heart stayed longing for the living God. He once said to me that he never understood me, except that I was a Christian and that I had a way of guarding myself without trying. But, it is the strategy of the Holy Spirit to guard the hearts and minds of those who love Christ, even in the midst of idol worship, strange mantras, and religions. Your Creator can use you with the zeal you have developed for the world for His good purpose and yours. He used Paul to spread the gospel with the same zeal that he had when he persecuted God's messengers.

I have learned that it is not how we start but how we finish. Man was created in God's image and is able to recreate and reason. In the book of Genesis, the word for image is from the Hebrew root word *tselem* (pronounced she'lem), which signifies a shade, resemblance, or replica.[159] We often err by focusing only on the physical resemblance and not the spiritual. It is our character that should be a reflection or resemblance of God's character. God commands us to "be holy, because I am holy."[160] Why? Because we are replicas of our Creator who always has a purpose for creating everything. If God is a God of purpose, and everything that exists was created by God for a purpose, then as replicas of God created in the image of God, we should be men and women of purpose! God also gave us the ability to recreate as He does. Man's delusion is that because he can reason and recreate as God does, he thinks that he is a little god. Actually, Jesus said that we can do the things that he did if we believe in Him, because we were created in His image. However, we need to realize that we are His creation and He gave the gift of creativity, intellect, reason, and wisdom to serve and worship Him. We were created to worship, and that is why some of us worship creation and not the Creator. We fashion objects of worship made of wood and stone. God wants our devotion and our worship, as He is able to give us everything we need to fulfill our purpose and be great at whatever we do and operate mightily as Gideon did.

Living with purpose is about walking in the will that your Creator destined for you, but first you have to understand who you are in relation to Him, and then apply that potent thought and reality to your life. You will find happiness and contentment in life when you live with purpose. Second-century A.D. Rome Emperor Marcus Aurelius once said, "The happiness of your life depends upon the quality of your thoughts, therefore guard accordingly and take care that you entertain no notions unsuitable to virtue, and reasonable nature."[161] Your thoughts about the Creator and, hence, about yourself, can bring you the happiness of life and bring contentment in whatever you do. When you give thought to that which is true and natural, such as your creation in the image of the purposeful Creator, then happiness will remain yours. Aurelius also stated that very little is needed to make a happy life, because we should "waste no more time talking about great souls and how they should be, but become one yourself. You will find rest from vain fancies if you do every act in life as though it were your last."[162] Living with purpose is about doing the thing your Creator called you to do with all that you have, as if it were the last thing on earth you had to do, no matter how great or small it may be. Hollywood legend James Dean once said, "Dream as if you will live forever, and live as if you only have today."[163] When you live with purpose, you will find happiness and contentment that no one will be able to comprehend, including yourself, and you will make a difference in the universe of mankind.

Chapter Ten
Vision Through the Veil

❧

"Where there is no vision [no redemptive revelation of God], the people perish; but he who keeps the law, blessed (happy, fortunate, and enviable) is he."

PROVERBS 29:18 AMP

"Vision is the ability to see things as they should be. If you try to function in any other way than faith, you will malfunction. That is why worry is ungodly and fear makes your vision short-circuit."

DR. MYLES MUNROE

"God takes good pleasure hiding things from us because He wants us to seek Him through His word, through His wonders, and through this world. Unveiled vision gives you the ability to see the revelation of His word and wonders."

RICARDO A. RICHARDSON

When Helen Keller, a blind and deaf prolific author and lecturer, was asked, "What is worse than being blind?" She responded, "Being able to see but having no vision." She also said, "Blindness has no limiting effect upon mental vision."[164] What then is vision? From a natural standpoint, vision is visual perception; the ability to see or eyesight. Vision is also foresight, and from a spiritual standpoint, a revelation or inspirational rendering of the future. Proverbs talks about foresight when Solomon states, "The wise look ahead to see what is coming, but fools deceive themselves."[165] Wouldn't it be an advantage to be able to look into the future and avoid all the mistakes and consequences from bad decisions in your life? God gave the gift of eyesight, but to those who seek and submit to Him, He has given spiritual vision, a glimpse of His future purpose.

A triathlon is a multisport endurance event consisting of swimming, cycling, and running in immediate succession over various distances. The tri-athlete competes for the fastest overall course completion time, including timed "transitions" between the individual swimming, biking, and running components. The triathlete knows the routes he has to run, ride, and swim, and he knows where the finish line is and what it looks like because he has been there before. He has practiced the event, going through the three segments of the race before the competition began. Similarly, God has the ability to show you where your finish line is and what it looks like, because He has been there before and can see your finish at the beginning. Each of us goes through life in our various jobs and relationships, but in each of our relationships, God provides a purpose to help fulfill our plans. Some people are in our lives for a time, season, or lifetime, and in each instance, they will be engaged in our purpose. We must understand their purpose and not control their reason for being there, as that is God's function. He will give you the vision to see Him as your purpose.

The Creator gives His creation everything needed for the fulfillment of our purpose. We need not develop those provisions we need on our own, neither must we be blessed with special vision to foresee the outcome of our lives. We search for God in temples, churches, and synagogues, but the God who made the world and everything in it is the Lord of heaven and earth and does not live in temples built by hands. He is not served by human hands—as if He needs anything—because He himself gives all people life and breath and everything else. From one man He made every nation of men that they should inhabit the whole earth; He determined the times set for them and the exact places where they should live. God did this so that men would seek Him, reach out for Him, and find Him; He is not far from each one of us. For in Him we live and move and have our being. As some of our own poets have said, we are his offspring.[166]

We are God's children along with His son, Jesus Christ, and everything that was available to Christ is available to all His offspring. Jesus' ultimate purpose was to die for all of God's children and to provide us with everything needed to fulfill our purpose. He is "the Alpha and the Omega, the First and the Last, the Beginning and the End,"[167] and everything in between!

When Moses asked God who he should tell the Israelites sent him when they were in bondage by Pharaoh, God replied: "I AM WHO I AM. This is what you are to say to the Israelites, I AM has sent me to you."[168] God is everything that His people need Him to be. He is what you need Him to be to fulfill your purpose. God reveals purpose and gives us vision to walk in our purpose and provides provision to fulfill our purpose. Whatever your purpose, God will be what you need in order to fulfill it. That is why Jesus said do not worry about your life or what you will eat, drink, or wear; seek your Father and he will provide all your needs. He clothes the lilies in the field, He feeds the birds, and He will feed you.[169]

It is such a wonderful thing to know God and live according to His word and will. But the only way you can learn, study, and train in the things of God is to study His word and learn about Him personally through your life experiences. God will communicate to us in many ways. No one can say for sure because God will reveal Himself to whomever He pleases, when, and as He pleases. The only way to the Father is through His Son, Jesus, the Savior, Lord, and Purpose of God toward mankind. The purposes of our hearts are like deep waters, but those with understanding will search God out so that He can reveal to us our purpose. Another proverb says, "It is the glory of God to conceal a thing, but the glory of kings is to search out the matter."[170] This verse encapsulates our discussion on searching God for a thing that we want. God knows all things. He is omniscient. There is nothing hidden from Him—no matter, no thing, and no purpose. Notice that in this passage it is the kings and queens that search out the matter. God sees each of us as His royal children, and your royalty qualifies you to have your purpose revealed and established. Jesus is the King of kings and Lord of lords, and those that believe in Him are adopted heirs to the kingdom. God created everyone, so we are all His creation, but we become heirs to His kingdom when we accept Jesus as Lord of our lives. This qualifies us for the revelation of purpose and all other mysteries of the Kingdom.

It is to God's glory to conceal things from us. He does this for several reasons. First, he wants us to seek Him in order to get to the core. God wants a relationship with us, and the Bible says He does not withhold anything that is good from us. God wants to teach us, instruct us, and guide us to a fulfilling eternal life in Christ Jesus. If He conceals those things that we not only want but need to be happy, our only option is to search Him out for revelation. That is why Jesus taught in parables and often said, "He who has ears, let them hear."[171] In other words, anyone who has ears to hear should listen and understand what I am saying to them. The prophet Isaiah also said, "Lead those who have eyes but are blind, who have ears but are deaf."[172]

Second, God wants to know how much we really want to know our purpose, to serve Him, and to have eternal life. Solomon could have asked for riches, wealth, fame, honor, and all the desires of men, but instead he asked God for wisdom. This moved God so much that He gave Solomon the very things he didn't ask for. God knew that with divine wisdom, Solomon would ultimately find riches, wealth, fame, and honor. How bad do you want to know your purpose? Will you seek God, your Creator for His revelation?

What is Jesus, the Son of the Living God, to you? He is the driving force of your purpose:

To the one searching for his purpose, He is the Revealer of purpose—
Proverbs 19:21, Proverbs 25:2, Matthew 7:7, Jeremiah 29:13.

To the athlete, He is the Prize—Philippians 3:14.

To the artist, He is altogether lovely—Song of Solomon 5:16.

To the architect, He is the chief Cornerstone—Psalm 118:22.

To the agriculturalist, He is the Fruit of the Spirit—Galatians 5:22.

To the astronomer, He is the bright Morning Star—Revelation 22:16.

To the baker, He is the Bread of Life—John 6:48.

To the banker, He is the Hidden Treasure—Matthew 13:44.

To the blind, He is the Vision—Psalm 146:8.

To the botanist, He is the Tree of Life—Genesis 2:9.

To the bride, He is the Bridegroom—Luke 5:35.

To the builder, He is the Sure Foundation—Isaiah 28:16.

To the carpenter, He is the Door—John 10:9.

To the clay, He is the Potter—Isaiah 64:8.

To the children, He is the Father—John 14:11.

To the doctor, He is the Great Physician—Luke 4:23.

To the educator, He is the Great Teacher—John 3:2.

To the explorer, He is the New Way—Hebrews 10:20.

To the farmer, He is Lord of the Harvest—Matthew 9:38.

To the firefighter, He is Living Water—John 7:38.

To the florist, He is the Rose of Sharon—Song of Solomon 2:1.

To the geologist, He is the Eternal Rock—Isaiah 26:4.

To the homeless, He is Shelter—Psalm 91:1.

To the horticulturist, He is the True Vine—John 15:1.

To the journalist, He is the Good News—Luke 2:10.

To the judge, He is the Righteous Judge—Psalm 7:11.

To the juror, He is the faithful Witness—Revelation 3:14.

To the jeweler, He is the Pearl—Matthew 13:46.

To the laborer, He is the Rest—Matthew 11:28.

To the lost, He is the Way— John 14:6.

To the lawyer, He is Fulfiller of the law—Matthew 5:17.

To the musician, He is a New Song—Psalm 40:3.

To the optometrist, He is Eyesight—Proverbs 29:13.

To the orphan, He is the Everlasting Father—Isaiah 9:6.

To the politician, He is the Government—Isaiah 9:6.

To the policeman, He is Safety—Proverbs 3:23.

To the philanthropist, He is the Indescribable Gift—2 Corinthians 9:15.

To the philosopher, He is the Wisdom of God—1 Corinthians 1:24.

To the patient, He is the Balm in Gilead—Jeremiah 8:22.

To the psychologist, He is the Wonderful Counselor—Isaiah 9:6.

To the preacher, He is the Word of God—John 1:1.

To the sculptor, He is the Living Stone—1 Peter 2:4.

To the soldier, He is his Strength and Shield—Psalm 28:7.

To the sower, He is the Seed—2 Corinthians 9:10.

To the student, He is Knowledge—Proverbs 1:7.

To the sinner, He is the Forgiver of sins—John 1:9.

To the teacher, He is All Knowledge – 1 Samuel 2:3.

To the widow, He is Defender—Psalm 68:5.

To the writer, He is the Author and Finisher of our faith—Hebrews 12:2.

To the Christian, He is the Son of the Living God, the Savior, the Creator, and the Giver of purpose.

In the opening chapter in the book of the Isaiah, the word *vision* is used: "The vision concerning Judah and Jerusalem that Isaiah, son of Amoz saw during the reigns of the kings of Judah."[173] The word as used in the Hebrew text is *chazon,* which translated means "divine revelation or sight into the future." On the other hand, the Hebrew word for eyesight, which is *reiyah,* is not used in this specific text. The book of Isaiah is about the revelation of events that would occur in the future, what God had planned and purposed for His people. A very interesting thing occurs in the sixth chapter of Isaiah. Isaiah had a vision of God seated on His throne, high and exalted. He realized that compared to the Almighty, he was nothing. This is a realization that we all must have. After seeing this vision, Isaiah responded, "Woe to me! I am ruined! For I am a man of unclean lips, and I live among a people of unclean lips, and my eyes have seen the King, the Lord Almighty."[174]

When you realize how awesome and powerful God is, you have a sense of reverence. Once you fully grasp that God is the Creator of all things past, present, and future, you will allow Him to lead your life and order your steps. I believe that the walk with God must start on your knees. I try to begin each day bowing before the Lord God Almighty as an act of reverence and acknowledgment of His sovereignty. This act allows me to begin each day in the right frame of mind, acknowledging that He is the Potter, and I am only the clay. Louis H. Evans once said, "Man is never so tall as when he kneels before God, never so great as when he humbles himself before God; and the man who kneels to God can stand up to anything."[175] Isaiah realized the awesome power of his Creator, and God immediately revealed His purpose to him. Once you and I realize that we serve a God of power and purpose, then we will be able to receive and operate in our purpose. Isaiah was a visionary and a prophet and saw a vision in the opening chapter of the book that bears his name. He had been prophesying about Judah and Jerusalem. But now, upon seeing a vision of the Almighty, he realized that his prophesying could not compare to the vision of God. But one of the angels touched his lips and took away Isaiah's guilt and sins. After this, God calls Isaiah to be a prophet to His people and tells him: "Go and tell this people: Be ever hearing but never understanding, be ever seeing but not perceiving."[176] The Creator gave Isaiah true vision, which would allow him to prophesy about God's plan and purpose for His people.

Vision through the veil is about spiritual vision, the ability to discern, and perception. The people's perception was tested as Jesus used parables to explain the kingdom of heaven to His disciples, followers, and critics. Many of them were unable to discern what He meant or see how the parable could relate to their lives. He spoke about earthly things with heavenly meanings, and many could not understand. At that time Jesus said, "I praise you, Father, Lord of heaven and earth, because you have hidden these things from the wise and learned and revealed them to little children. Yes, Father, for this is what you were pleased to do. All things have been committed to me by my Father."[177] Eugene Peterson's The Message translation says it this way: "Thank you Father, Lord of heaven and earth. You've concealed your ways from sophisticates and know-it-alls, but spelled them out clearly to ordinary people. Yes, Father, that's the way you like to work." Jesus clearly gives us a picture of how God takes pleasure in hiding things from us so we can seek Him to have them revealed. Jesus also says nothing is hidden from Him because He knows the Father and the Father knows Him, so he knows everything there is to know about you, especially your purpose. Once we accept Jesus as Lord, He reveals everything to us that the Father has hidden, including our purpose.

Our sight is finite, but God's sight is infinite. We cannot see things as He does with our natural vision, and hence we cannot comprehend or understand the things that are hidden from us. Many of us focus on the things we can see, touch, and feel. The word *hidden* in the Greek is "kruptows," which means to conceal with the emphasis that the concealment began at an earlier point and is continuing into the future. Jesus is *continually* trying to get His followers to see and understand: "He who has eyes, let him see." He said that he came to give sight to the blind, which was hard for many of the people to visualize, no pun intended. Jesus literally gave sight to those with natural blindness, but he also gave sight to those with spiritual blindness, giving them vision behind the veil. Additionally, his statement showed that he made a distinction between natural and spiritual sight. Spiritual sight is perception and understanding revealed only by God. He wants us to rely on our spiritual senses, which gives us spiritual vision. God is hidden from us because He desires for us to see (seek) Him through His word, through His world, and through His wonders.

The keen point Jesus makes about hiding the knowledge of God is directed to the wise and learned. He is stating here that the wise and learned believe they have vast knowledge, but wisdom and knowledge come from the Father. There is worldly wisdom and spiritual wisdom, as there is worldly vision and spiritual vision. The wisdom of this world is foolishness in God's sight. "As it is written, 'He catches the wise in their craftiness;' and again, 'The Lord knows that the thoughts of the wise are futile.'"[178] The wise cannot know God simply by reading and studying the things of the world. Jesus is saying that some people can know of God but still not know Him personally. The psalmist says that His ways and thoughts are higher than ours. This suggests that no earthly wisdom can compare to His heavenly wisdom. And no matter how great we may think we are, God's thoughts are always higher. Conversely, if we think little of ourselves, He can elevate our thinking.

Jesus spoke in parables so that the people would apply themselves to understanding the mysteries of the kingdom of heaven. "The knowledge of the secrets of the kingdom of heaven has been given to you, but not to them. Whoever has will be given more, and he will have abundance. Whoever does not have, even what he has will be taken from him. This is why I speak to them in parables: 'Though seeing, they do not see; though hearing, they do not hear or understand.'"[179] And God spoke through Isaiah: "You shall indeed hear but never understand, and you shall indeed see but never perceive. For this people's heart has grown dull, and their ears are heavy of hearing, and their eyes they have closed, lest they should perceive with their eyes, and hear with their ears, and understand with their heart, and turn for me to heal them."[180] As it was in days past, so it is today. God wants us to hear His word, listen, and understand so that we can achieve fulfillment in life and in our purpose.

God hides his purpose until you are ready to receive it and He is ready to reveal it. He is interested in our perception and discernment. Solomon asked God for wisdom and a discerning heart, and God granted it to him. The psalmist says that wisdom calls to all a desire to receive it. When you ask God for wisdom and understanding, He gives it freely as well as the tangible things you didn't ask for. Wisdom allows you to stand in the presence of God and on the side of His purpose. There are two places you can stand: on the side of God's purpose or on the side of man's plans. What do I mean? Our parents plan our lives for us until we are able to plan for ourselves. They plan our involvement in sports, arts, music, theater, schools, careers, and some even plan whom we will marry and where we will live as adults. Some parents are content to pass their plans onto you and influence the choices that you make henceforth and forevermore. We all stand on our plans or the plans of someone else.

God understands this concept and the intellectual mind of man. That is why he says, "Many are the plans in a man's heart, but it is the Lord's purpose that prevails."[181] God is always in charge, whether we depend on our own plans and desires or His. Pharaoh had no intention of letting the Israelites go and hardened his heart every time Moses requested their release. In fact, the Bible says that God hardened his heart. The same can be said for Joseph's brothers. Their plan was to kill Joseph, but they changed their minds and sold him into slavery instead. God used the plan of man for the purpose of Joseph. He will use the plans of people who are in your life to fulfill the purpose for your life. So even though your parents, spouse, or friends try to plan and run your life, God will use those plans for His purpose in your life if you seek and serve Him.

An associate of mine, Donahue Peebles, is an example of using vision, passion, and drive to propel his purpose to uncommon places. His purpose and drive in life propelled him to be one of the most successful entrepreneurs in America. As he states in his book, *The Peebles Principle*, he was not born with a silver spoon in his mouth, but by the time he was twenty-seven, he was a multimillionaire, and by the time he was forty-five, he was worth more than a quarter of a billion dollars.[182] The financial blessing he received did not define him, and he remains one of the most humble individuals that I have met. He coaches his son's basketball team, and he established a capital fund to invest in young entrepreneurs' new business ventures. He gives back to the various communities that are near his hotel developments.

Don built a real estate empire and is the CEO of The Peebles Corporation, a successful real estate development company. One of his principles is turning vinegar into wine, as setbacks are opportunities in disguise. In other words, no matter what obstacle or setback you encounter, it is only an opportunity for your purpose to become more potent. Your purpose will make room for you to be in uncommon places doing uncommon things. So Pebbles saw setbacks as opportunities that propelled him to higher ground and gave his deals a new dynamic that did not seem viable before. When you stay focused and determined and resolve to succeed, your purpose will give you another vision, vantage point, and perspective that only you will be able to see and capitalize upon.

Vision is also about seeing what others do not. It may be a better perspective or seeing an opportunity. For example, one young man, Pierre Omidyar, saw an opportunity that many could not fathom. Omidyar, a software programmer, wrote software for his company, Auctionweb. He was amazed when the first item sold was a broken laser pointer from a collector. He changed the name of the company to eBay, and the rest is history. He saw the passion that people had to collect "ordinary" items, so he developed eBay as a portal for buying and selling. Omidyar saw an opportunity and turned that opportunity into a multibillion-dollar company. In 2002, eBay acquired the online payment-processing firm PayPal, which it uses to process its own eBay sales as well as processing payment transactions for the general public. What some people see as a problem, others see as an opportunity. It is all about perspective and attitude. A quote that I believe embodies vision, perception, and attitude is by Author Wayne Dyer, who says, "Change the way you look at things, and the things you look at will change."[183]

Omidyar had a purpose that led him to start eBay so that he could provide funding for his true passion, which is philanthropy. In 2005, the Omidyars donated $100 million—the largest single gift in university history—to Tufts to create the Omidyar-Tufts Micfrofinance Fund. The Omidyar Network has committed more than $383 million internationally to organizations to spark broad, positive social change.[184] Omidyar also supports the development of an application that allows users to track damage from oil spills in the Gulf of Mexico and to locate trapped survivors of the 2010 earthquake in Haiti. In 2010, Omidyar joined Microsoft founder Bill Gates and Warren Buffet on the list of billionaires who pledged to donate at least half of their wealth to charity. In 2014, *Forbes* estimated Omidyar's net worth at $8 billion. Omidyar has purpose to use his wealth to affect change in the lives of people internationally, a very admirable and noble endeavor.

We may not have billions of dollars like the Omidyars and Buffets of the world, but there are meaningful causes we can all participate in to affect positive change in people's lives. Your purpose may not be tied to giving money, but it is tied to giving. Giving what? Giving your time or talent. Your purpose has to be tied to giving. God's purpose to redeem the world was tied to giving His Son, Jesus, who gave of himself to bring us closer to God, our Creator. As parents, it is our job to teach our children to give and be mindful of others less fortunate than us. We do not neglect our duty to expose them to education, arts, music, sports, and all other facets of life, but it is also our responsibility to educate them about purpose and instill in them a belief that their existence is much more about their true identity (in Christ) than developing a reputation. It is also not our job to choose their purpose or plan their life for them. Our responsibility is to teach them about their Creator, who possesses the purpose for their lives, and allow them to operate in His knowledge.

I grew up playing basketball in the Bahamas and won a scholarship to St. John's University. Like most players, I thought that I had the ability to make it to the NBA. I wanted this dream to be my son's also. The reality is that it never happened for me, although I got involved in the business of basketball as CEO of the Continental Basketball Association, which operated for more than 60 years, and was once the developmental league to the NBA. My son met several current and former NBA players who encouraged him to practice hard and maybe one day he would fulfill his father's dream.

As coach of Zion's third-grade basketball team, I would get so frustrated because I knew that he understood what to do in games, but he would forget to box out, or rebound with two hands, or not shoot a jump shot the right way. I would think to myself, "I did not forget how to play when I was nine years old!" But my mother reminded me that I was not serious about the game until much later. I would clown on the court and not focus. Then something hit me. Why was I getting so frustrated about how Zion plays? He is giving his best and working hard to compete. Is it worth chastising him and making him feel like he could not please me? How many times have I fallen short of what God expected of me? Like Gideon, I needed proof of His word, needed encouragement, and continually doubted. But, God showed unimaginable patience and grace with me. It finally dawned on me that I am not responsible for choosing Zion's or any of my children's purpose. My responsibility is to expose them to the positive things in life, help them develop their talents, and then allow God to influence their purpose by giving them passion for it.

A quote often attributed to Harvey Mackay, business development author and columnist, states, "Find something that you love to do and you will never have to work a day in your life." When you do what you love and operate in your purpose, you will do it not for financial gain, but personal satisfaction. Love is the foundation of living life with purpose. Our Creator has a purpose for sending His Son, Jesus, to redeem mankind from sin, but what was the most noted reason God gave this gift to us? The same reason that we give gifts to family members and friends on Christmas and birthdays; love! We give gifts to those we love! God gave us Jesus as a gift because of His love! For God so loved the world that he gave, that whosoever believe shall have life! God didn't give out of obligation, duty, or guilt. He gave out of love. Likewise, God gives us our purpose because He loves us.

The veil is something that hinders our vision. It may be the circumstances and issues of life, relationships, fear, hardships, trials, money, fame, reputation, pride, and many other issues. This veil blinds us from seeing our purpose and our full potential. The fact that we cannot see it does not mean it does not exist. Solomon was not hung up on being king, his reputation, or how much money or wisdom he had; he was focused on building the temple of God for the glory of God. There was no veil hindering his vision to fulfill his project for God. Moses' veil was life as the prince of Egypt. At first it was conditioning him to be blind to the hardships of his fellow Hebrews. I am sure that he saw his people struggle in slavery while he ate at the king's table. Then while witnessing his fellow Hebrew's assault, he saw through the veil and came to his rescue. He forgot about his position as prince and defended his Hebrew brother. God later appeared to Moses in the burning bush and gave him the purpose for his life. God then purposed Moses to deliver the Israelites from Pharaoh and take them to the entrance of the Promised Land. I believe that when Moses fled after he killed the Egyptian, he began to reflect on the meaning of his life and search for his purpose. God met Moses at that point and revealed not only Himself but also Moses' purpose.

In 2008, I visited New Delhi, India on a business trip and saw some beautiful buildings and people. The women there are beautiful, but most of them cover their faces and eyes. I asked one of my associates why they hide themselves, and he said it is because they do not want to be exposed to men. And if they are exposed, some of them paint red dots on their foreheads indicating that they are married and not available to men not chosen for them. The veils covering their faces are so thin that they can see outside but not be fully seen.

We also want to hide behind the veils in our lives, but like many of the Indian women, we should begin to see through our veils. What is your veil? Is it fear? Is it disbelief? What hinders you from the promise of your purpose? From pursuing that which you love? God can remove the veil and give you vision to see yourself as He sees you and to see your purpose as He sees it. Remember, a person only sees what you do, but God sees the reason why.

Chapter Eleven

Getting to the Core

ཚོ

"Many are the plans of a man's heart; but it is the Lord's purpose that prevails."

PROVERBS 19:21

"I am a firm believer that the Lord sometimes has to short-circuit even our best plans for our benefit."

TONY DUNGY

"A self-centered man searches externally for his plans in life, but a God-centered man searches internally for God's purpose and allows his purpose to find and identify him. A plan outside of this is fruitless."

RICARDO A. RICHARDSON

Many of us make plans to accomplish our goals in life, and some of us do just that, either with a level of satisfaction or discontent. I have made many plans about my life—whom I would marry, where I would live, how much money I would earn by a certain age. I found little satisfaction and contentment in my plans, as they were all self-centered. The difference between finding satisfaction or dissatisfaction in what we do in life is love, purpose, and passion. If we find that which we love, God uses that love and passion to fuel the purpose in our lives. He is the one that gives us the purpose that will define our lives and bring contentment. God is so powerful that He can take our plans, regardless if they fail or succeed, and absorb them into His purpose for our lives and the lives of others.

God's ultimate purpose is for His kingdom culture to exist on earth. That is why He made it and made us. He began with a garden called Eden and will end with a city of gold. Solomon received the purpose from God to build His first house of worship. Then he built his own palace after that. All over the world, churches, temples, synagogues, and houses of God are being built, along with various cities ruled by governments and private citizens. God's model for a holy city is being duplicated around the world. The first temple was built, and God put His name there. The city was built around the temple of God so that He could dwell with the people, and consecrate not only the temple, but the people and the city, too. But God told Solomon that He would reject the temple, and consequently the city and its citizens, if they did not follow Him:

> I have heard the prayer and plea you have made before me; I have consecrated this temple, which you have built, by putting my Name there forever. My eyes and my heart will always be there. As for you, if you walk before me in integrity of heart and uprightness, as David your father did, and do all I command and observe my decrees and laws, I will establish your royal throne over Israel forever, as I promised David your father when I said, 'You shall never fail to have a man on the throne of Israel.' But if you or your sons turn away from me and do not observe the commands and decrees I have given you and go off to serve other gods and worship them, then I will cut off Israel from the land I have given them and will reject this temple I have consecrated for my Name. Israel will then become a byword and an object of ridicule among all peoples. And though this temple is now imposing, all who pass by will be appalled and will scoff and say, 'Why has the Lord done such a thing to this land and to this temple?' People will answer, 'Because they have forsaken the Lord their God, who brought their fathers out of Egypt, and have embraced other gods, worshiping and serving them—that is why the Lord brought all this disaster on them.[185]

We see God's promises to Solomon regarding the building of the temple, which was a purpose He established for Solomon. God demonstrated His approval by putting His name on Solomon's purpose. Is God's name on your purpose? Additionally, He gave a promise to Solomon and to us that if we keep His word, our descendants would be blessed. This is what God wants for you and me: to seek Him, keep His laws, and honor Him. How do we show honor? By submitting to God and allowing Him to reveal His purpose to us as opposed to following our own plans.

Within the cities of God, everyone has a purpose and a role to play. Some may be masons, architects, planners, florists, administrators, government leaders, or teachers. There is a purpose for all to exist and function in the city within the domains of society, among which are religion, agriculture, business, arts, education, architecture, technology, and government. God does not separate church, business, arts, technology, government, and other domains in his kingdom. There is no secular-sacred divide, as God is the Creator of all things. In fact, Isaiah stated, "For to us a child is born, to us a son is given, and the government will be on his shoulders. And he will be called Wonderful Counselor, Mighty God, Everlasting Father, Prince of Peace."[186] It does not say the church or synagogue would be on his shoulders, but the government. The government is the organization that supposes to hold society together. It regulates with laws and decrees, provides protection through police and fire stations, and provides education through schools. God exists in government and every other domain of society. Many have taught the separation between church and state, but there is no such divide. We try to create a box to fit God into so we can feel that we are in some kind of control. By limiting the Creator to religion, we try to separate business, government, and other domains of society under our sole control. It is human fallacy that makes us believe we can limit an infinite God to a finite area of our lives, like religion. When you realize and accept that God exists in your business, school, government, home, and in every area of life, then you can readily accept His purpose for your life, because His purpose for you encompasses all these domains. God does not only call people to be pastors, deacons, or church administrators. He also calls doctors, teachers, politicians, mentors, and social workers. However, he does call everyone to teach their children, family, and others about Him so that they, too, can find purpose and fulfillment in their lives.

God wants you to follow your heart and find what you love to do, not for money because money does not motivate God; money motivates man. Solomon understood this and struck at the very heart of God when he asked God for a discerning heart. Because Solomon asked for that which God valued, he also received what man valued, namely money, power, and fame. God realizes that these things are valuable to man. He just wants us to continue to worship Him instead of worshiping them. That is why Jesus said, "No one can serve two masters. Either he will hate the one and love the other, or he will be devoted to the one and despise the other. You cannot serve both God and money."[187] God knows that the love of money is what causes men to sin, not money itself. They worship money and would do anything to have it, including destroying other people's lives. The psalmist says, "Do not trust in extortion or take pride in stolen goods; though your riches increase, do not set your heart on them."[188]

Ricardo Richardson

This was what Jesus referred to when he said not to love money; but people devise all sorts of plans and schemes to get money. One of the largest illegal money schemes was orchestrated by Bernie Madoff, the Wall Street financier who embezzled more than $150 billion of his investors' money. He received a 150-year prison sentence for this crime. The scheme ruined thousands of people's lives, caused individual victims to not be able to support their families, to lose their physical and mental health, and even commit suicide. Madoff built his plans to succeed, but they were built on lies, deceit, and misrepresentations. He built his plans on foundations that were not solid, and as a result, they did not succeed. Jesus taught about building plans on solid ground. He said,

> Therefore, everyone who hears these words of mine and puts them into practice is like a wise man who built his house on the rock. The rain came down, the streams rose, and the winds blew and beat against that house; yet it did not fall, because it had its foundation on the rock. But everyone who hears these words of mine and does not put them into practice is like a foolish man who built his house on sand. The rain came down, the streams rose, and the winds blew and beat against that house, and it fell with a great crash.[189]

We should listen to the words of the Creator and build our house, our plans, on His purpose—the most solid ground that exists. We should follow His word and be obedient, and the spiritual, emotional, physical, and financial blessings will naturally follow. God will manifest in each of us His blessings as we fulfill our love for service to bring about a kingdom culture in our lives.

I had plans of my own, and I mapped out in detail what my life would be like ten, even twenty years after I graduated from college, but my plans were melded into God's purpose for my life. The temperature on campus was subzero, and I was experiencing something referred to as culture shock. I grew up in the Bahamas, a warm and sunny archipelago of islands. I had never experienced anything like what I was going through in Minnesota my first winter at college. It was so cold on campus that I would wear layers of long johns under more layers of clothing. During the winter, students would limit their movements and stay confined to the dormitories to stay warm, and the only thing we could do was study, which was probably why so many of us were dedicated to our books.

I had received a basketball scholarship and financial aid to attend St. John's University. I was one of the most promising young basketball players in the Bahamas, and everyone, including me, planned my future as a professional basketball player. I averaged more than thirty points per game my senior year at St. Augustine's in Nassau. I played against NBA players during summer breaks, so I believed that my skills were developing into something that would propel me to the NBA. My plan was to go to college, play basketball, and one day be drafted into the NBA.

Derek Wilson, one of my best friends, had similar plans, but his was to play in the NFL. Both of us decided that this was the only course we would endeavor to pursue, because it seemed right to us. He decided to go to Mississippi and later transferred to Idaho State, where he played football. I wanted to go to St. John's because I had heard a lot about the school. Too late, I discovered that I was enrolled in the wrong St. John's. Mine was not the one known for its athletics but its academics. My St. John's is located in Collegeville, Minnesota, not New York. The St. John's I thought I was enrolling in is an NCAA Division I school that rivaled Georgetown and other Big East schools. The St. John's I attended was a NCAA Division III school, a private institution with an impressive academic record. I'd had the opportunity to go to Drake University, a Division I school in Iowa, but I chose St. John's instead. My plans were to play professional basketball, but God had another purpose for me. He allowed my plans to attend the St. John's that I wanted to be absorbed by His purpose to attend the St. John's that He wanted me to.

There were several people at St. John's who had a profound impact on my life. Jim Smith, my head basketball coach, had more than 700 wins and is among the top coaches in winnings on any NCAA level. He was a mentor on and off the basketball court. I met a math professor, Dr. Robert Dumonceaux, who became a mentor and friend. This increased my love for math, and I later graduated with a degree in mathematics and statistics. Roger Young, an administrator, introduced me to J. Patrick Rooney, who mentored me in business and gave me my first job as an actuary right out of college.

My plans to play professional sports were interrupted by God's purpose for my life. Like any parent or guardian, our Father God wants us to acquire as much wisdom, knowledge, and education as possible. The more knowledge we acquire, the better equipped we are to instruct others, increase productivity through our work, and improve quality of life for ourselves and for others. But in addition to learning about our work and life, He expects us to learn about Him as well. Education is a key that can open doors of opportunity and provide its possessor the ability to excel in their respective fields. The opportunities in life always come from the Creator, but the education and knowledge is a requirement to take full advantage of the opportunity.

The founder of eBay was educated as a computer software programmer, and when the opportunity came to trade collectibles via the Internet, he was able to develop the software needed. He could still have capitalized on the opportunity, but he would have had to find someone else educated in the field of programming who could add the same if not more value to the opportunity than he possessed. But having knowledge yourself accelerates the possibility of success. I chose education because it was a long shot for me to make the NBA, especially playing for a smaller university. I knew that education would be a key that would unlock doors of opportunity for me that outnumbered the doors that sports could open. I graduated and moved back home to the Bahamas where job opportunities for a person with a degree in mathematics were limited to teaching. I believe teaching is a very noble profession, and my mother taught math and English and is now a primary school principal, but I did not have a desire to teach, as this was not a part of my plan or my purpose.

After graduation, I applied to Indianapolis-based Golden Rule Insurance Company, founded by insurance mogul J. Patrick Rooney. Pat was an alumnus of St. John's and operated a multimillion-dollar individual life and health insurance company. I learned a valuable lesson about mentorship when I attended St. John's. Dr. Dumonceaux, my math professor who allowed me to be a part of his life beyond the halls of the university, mentored me in academics and in life. The one thing that I realized is that humility is very important in mentorship. As I continued my career, I would encounter leaders in their respective industries, and I would humble myself and ask them for guidance and for them to mentor me in that specific field. This is exactly the way God wants us to approach Him, with humility, asking for Him to lead us, instruct us, and reveal to us what we need to uncover our purpose.

Golden Rule Insurance Company was always looking for actuaries, and because I had a degree in mathematics, I was qualified to apply. An actuary develops the rates of the insured groups based on statistics, loss rations, premiums, and health risk. I would essentially assign risk to a particular group of insureds. I met with Pat Rooney, and he hired me on the spot, offering me the position of assistant actuary pending the approval of my work visa. When I joined Golden Rule, I asked Pat to mentor me in the insurance business. I remember the advice Pat gave me on a variety of issues was always on target. He became more than my employer; he became a father figure and friend. He would entertain my mother and Aunt Vivia when they visited me from the Bahamas each year, inviting them to his house for dinner. On his desk were photos of all his children, grand-children, great-grandchildren—and my daughter, Raven. I would smile when I entered into his office for our private mentoring lunch meetings, because I could always spot my little girl among all the pictures that graced his desk; she was the one who was sun-kissed.

It took about four months to get approved for my US work permit, and during that time, I worked in the Bahamas painting the inside of office buildings. This was a very humbling experience and would prove to be the first of many such instances. I recalled a young man saying to me, "You must be the most edu-cated painter I have ever met." I never gave up hope that my work visa would be approved, but it seemed like an eternity. I remember thinking of alternative plans I would pursue if this opportunity fell through. Everyone around me except my family thought that it would be almost impossible for me to work at a major insurance company in Indiana, so far from home. But when God has a purpose for your life, no one and nothing can stop it from being manifested.

Like the football timing play, the blessings had been thrown to another loca-tion, and I would not be in position to receive them while living in the Bahamas. God may arrange your blessing in another place and you have to reposition your-self to receive it. My plans were to move to Indianapolis, work as an actuary, then return home to work for the National Insurance Board of the Bahamas. I met with the administrator and told them of my plans to work in the United States for three years and then return home, but that plan never manifested. I did work for Golden Rule for three years but left to take a position with Roadway Global Air, the air-freight logistic company of Fortune 500 transportation company YRC Roadway. I became the senior forecast analyst in the short time I was there, and then got an offer to join Eclipse Consulting Group as vice president of operations. Eclipse had developed software to administrate medical savings accounts (MSAs), the new healthcare savings plans pioneered by my mentor and friend, Pat Rooney and

Golden Rule Insurance. At the time, this was a huge deal because managed health-care maintenance organizations (HMOs) were just becoming popular. Eclipse needed me to develop a relationship with Golden Rule, the largest underwriter of MSAs, as their plans for an audience with Pat Rooney could never be realized. I facilitated the meeting and during our discussions, we discovered that the health-care system was much more broken than we anticipated and was one of the slow-est industries open to technology. As a result, Eclipse developed an electronic claims administration system to provide accurate insured data, and settle health-care provider claims and payer adjudication. This system not only electronically administrated MSAs but all healthcare products, and out of this, RealMed Corpo-ration was born. RealMed assembled some of the biggest players in healthcare: Anthem Blue Cross Blue Shield, CIT Financial Group, Johnson & Johnson Devel-opment Corporation, and Gemplus, a smartcard manufacturer. I was the executive vice president and chief operating officer of RealMed at twenty-seven years of age.

Everything I learned from Pat Rooney, I used in the boardroom. Pat had taken me to Washington, DC a few years prior to meet with Democratic and GOP mem-bers to discuss the validity of MSAs for patient choice in healthcare services. He'd introduced me as his business associate, which exposed me to another level of business and politics. Since then, I have made several trips to Washington, one of them to launch RealMed Corporation at the National Press Club. I worked for RealMed as the executive VP and COO until I took a stance for Gemplus Corpo-ration, the seed investors in RealMed. I challenged the CFO of the company for the use of investor funds, which ended in my departure.

There were questions from the French investors about the use of funds, and since I was the point person, I would field all the questions surrounding the invest-ment. RealMed had planned to go public as an exit strategy for the investors and shareholders. The company wanted to establish a value of the stock so that they would stage an initial public offering (IPO) with at least that stated value. I was used to make this happen. I remember one meeting at a local restaurant with the RealMed CEO, who offered to buy back my stock because he claimed that he felt sorry for what I went through. I was not employed at the time and could have really used the money, but something didn't feel right. I did not go through with the sale to him, and two weeks later I discovered that CIT Group, a billion-dollar company, was acquiring controlling interest in the company; my stock would now be worth millions of dollars. The initial offer to sell was about a few thousand dollars.

This is one of several issues involving partners whom I trusted. I would continually put my complete trust in man, and the result was always the same; loss of wealth and disappointment. This was a valuable lesson that I should have learned from but that repeated itself several times with other companies and partners.

The RealMed experience was a valuable one. I was young and making more money than I had ever imagined, and I had friends from the Bahamas who had relocated to Indianapolis, where I resided. I gave them a condo and vehicles to drive free of charge, and sent money back to their families. I was living the life, and my friends praised me for my advancement in business. I started believing them that my plans and my dynamic networking abilities had put me in the lofty position that I was in. I started believing that nothing was out of my reach. My net worth was close to $10 million, and I lived in a million-dollar home across from the former ambassador to Mexico. I was only twenty-seven years of age, the youngest person on the board of directors. I associated with major members of the House of Representatives on Capitol Hill and international investment bankers from the United States, France, and Switzerland. These were the relationships that I thought would propel me to success, but none of them actually did. I was depending on men to open doors for me and support my advancement in my career and life. I thought my plans were working, but it all came tumbling down on me.

I was on top of the world in 1997. I knew several individuals who held stock options and became instant multimillionaires during the technology IPO boom. Mark Cuban, owner of the Dallas Mavericks, had acquired his wealth through the sale of public stock, and I was planning on becoming wealthy the same way. I was waiting for my payday, but it all came crashing down a year later when the technology market crashed. RealMed was scheduled to go public in the year 2000, when the NASDAQ experienced what some call the dot-com or IT bubble.[190] Technology stocks soared from 1998 to 2000, where technology equity value rose rapidly from the Internet sector. Many Internet companies that did not have "real" or hard assets saw market capitalization in the billions. America Online (AOL) was one of the beneficiaries of the Internet sector and, as a result, made a bid to buy Time Warner, a traditional company. AOL was able to do this because its market capitalization or value was much greater than Time Warner's at the time, even though Time Warner had more tangible, fixed assets. The dot-com bubble crash wiped out $5 trillion in market value of technology companies from March 2000 to October 2002.[191] RealMed was scheduled to launch its IPO in 2000, but management did not proceed due to the massive sell-offs and index decline in NASDAQ. I watched as my assets in the company dropped in value to virtually nothing. My ego needed to be in check, and this was the beginning of the struggle to start my own business and continue to build plans to gain power and wealth.

I devised another plan: I'd go into business for myself. I started another technology company, and later joined the American Basketball Association (ABA) as a general manager for one of their teams. One of my business associates, a CEO of the largest advertising agency in Indianapolis, introduced me to the CEO of the ABA. He knew I loved basketball and thought this would be a good opportunity for me. He was one of the original owners of the Indiana team, along with the league CEO and a local politician. I met the CEO, and his enthusiasm, salesmanship, and attitude about the league and team convinced me to get involved with them. But the league was in a crisis situation, and I did not realize this until I accepted the position. The next day, I visited the team at a hotel to meet the players and head coach, only to discover annual bills had not been paid, the head coach had resigned, and the players were getting thrown out of the hotel. At this point, I was wondering what I had gotten myself into. When I looked at those players, I saw myself, because this was a plan I'd had for myself coming out of college. Many of these players didn't have a second option. I met with the players that day by the pool and assured them that I would not quit on them and that we would have a season. I had limited capital, but I had a passion for basketball. I asked them who they would want to coach them and they told me Freddie Lewis, a former Indiana Pacer.

Freddie had wanted to coach the team but had been hired as a basketball scout instead. This was an opportunity that he'd been awaiting. I called him and he drove from Pennsylvania to meet with me. We immediately connected, and I hired him as head coach. I then negotiated a deal for furnished apartments and moved the players and coaches there. When I visited the team office, I found that everyone had quit, and the merchandise guy and I were the only ones left. I later discovered that the team owed most of their prior vendors, including the Fieldhouse where the team played its home games. I tried to renegotiate a deal with the venue, but they refused to accept any offers from the team or league. I explained my dilemma to Coach Lewis, and he told me the original Indiana Pacers team had played in the Pepsi Coliseum. I thought this would be a great marketing move and would bring back nostalgia for the team. I met with the general manager of the Coliseum, and immediately he expressed his discontent. They had had past dealings, and he was not shy about demonstrating that he was not in support of the team playing there. I had made some political connections in the city and called on them for support. The Pepsi Coliseum is a part of the Indiana State Fairgrounds, so as a public facility, they could not deny a tenant that wanted to rent the facility. They could, however, make it extremely difficult, which they did.

The Indianapolis Ice hockey team played there and they got most, if not all of the weekend dates. The Coliseum charged us almost three times the amount that the Fieldhouse had charged, and I had to present a cashier's check by noon on game day or the building would be closed. I remember one cold evening (I was traveling out of town that day and could not drop the cashier's check off to the office) when I got a call that the doors were locked! Fans that came to the game were standing out in the cold and could not get in. We finally were able to open the doors the hour I arrived. The difficulties and struggles kept mounting on top of my plans.

There were so many roadblocks during my days with the ABA, but I stuck with it. I was determined to transform this league into a professional one and gave up everything to achieve that goal. I leveraged my home, stocks, vehicles, and all my assets to borrow money to pay players and vendors. I received part ownership in the team, which in the end was so devalued that I could not recoup even a small portion of my investment. To help offset some of the loss, I received full ownership in two other franchises, but their value was only a fraction of what I had already invested. I just wanted to make it through the season and give the players an opportunity to be called up to the NBA or receive an overseas contract. I operated as a one-person staff, scheduling the games, road trips, hotel accommodations, marketing and sales, and sports interviews with local news media. I remember that at every meeting I had with local vendors and TV stations, the first thing I did was apologize for what had happened in the past and give my assurance that it would not happen again. By the end of the season, I had revamped the financial model and business model of the team, which would be used by the league office and all teams the following years.

I did not continue as a team owner because of the loss I had suffered, but later got an offer to be involved at the league level. I did not want new owners to have to go through what I had, and I knew that the league and teams could be profitable if the business model was improved. The CEO asked me to be the VP of operations and implement the financial and business model that I used for the Indiana team. I saw this as an opportunity to help other new franchises capitalize on the opportunity and help them avoid all the obstacles with minor league professional ownership. My responsibilities included visiting the potential new city and team owner, negotiating the venue lease, meeting with potential investors, and writing a team-specific business and marketing plan. We had several very good team operations. The Indiana team was owned by a sports enthusiast devoted to his team's success. He understood not only the game of basketball but the business of basketball. He hired a former Indiana Hoosier and NBA player as head coach, and they put together a fantastic season, winning more than 17 straight games.

Indiana, San Jose, Southern California, and Arkansas were some of the model teams I developed, although there were several other teams that were well-managed and had dedicated owners. I recommended that the Arkansas owner hire Otis Birdsong, former NBA All-Star, as general manager. Otis had a great basketball and business mind, and together we built one of the most successful minor-league franchises in professional basketball. We interviewed former NBA New York Knicks legend Nate "Tiny" Archibald for head coach of the team, but later hired a former Arkansas college coach. The Arkansas Rimrockers were loved by the city. The team won the championship in front of more than 14,000 home fans that attended the game.

The following year the team moved to the NBA Developmental League. I had wanted this franchise as a model team for others to follow, and the team, along with the other solid franchises, wanted to make changes at the league level. The problem we had was that many expansion teams were undercapitalized. They ran poor franchises and did not show up for games, did not have proper uniforms or home venues, or played in local recreation centers. It was embarrassing at times. I was able to develop another franchise similar to Arkansas the following year in south Florida. The Florida Pitbulls, led by NBA Miami Heat All-Star guard Tim Hardaway, was co-owned by ex-NFL New York Jets quarterback Jay Fiedler. The opening game saw more than 5000 fans in attendance at the beautiful Bank

Atlantic arena, but disagreement with owners, league management, and operations forced many teams to fold midway in the season.

Additionally, I put together the first major league sponsorship deal. The team model, league model, and sponsorships were beginning to position the league as an alternative for young players that were not drafted to the NBA and did not want to go overseas to play professionally. After the disagreements with league owners, no shows, continued rescheduling of missed games, and unprofessional and undercapitalized ball clubs, I decided that I could not change the culture of the league, so I resigned and joined the Continental Basketball Association (CBA), the oldest professional basketball league, dating back to 1946. Half of the CBA teams, the top franchises, joined the D-League. I spent two years with the CBA as the CEO of CBA Enterprises, the marketing, management, and developmental arm of the league. I launched an initiative to establish CBA leagues worldwide. I met with the CEO of Basketball Canada in Toronto, the Minister of Sports in the Bahamas, and billionaire Mexican businessman, Mr. Jorge Vergara of Chivas Soccer Club in Guadalajara, Mexico. My vision and plan was to establish a global basketball community similar to what the NBA is currently doing in China, Europe, and other countries. Again, all my plans, hard work, and dedication to the ABA league were not met with fairness by former partners and associates. This did not deter me from continuing my plan to gain wealth, prestige, and position, and I believed that I had developed the skills to do so. I was not focused on what God wanted for me, only what I wanted for myself, what I thought was in my own plans and my best interest.

I later started a marketing and business management consulting company. I have worked with companies in healthcare, technology, professional sports, construction management, finance, and manufacturing, and I kept coming up against unethical partners who used my skills and then tried to take advantage of me. I also became involved with pastors who were all about lining their pockets and promoting their own agendas. This opened my eyes. The first lesson happened repeatedly until I learned from it. But in every situation and business partnership I was involved in, I was able to develop additional skills that I took with me to the next opportunity.

By this time, I was an unofficial attorney, accountant, salesman, promoter, and computer administrator because of the knowledge that I had received over the years. I was educated in many fields, which God was planning to use for a purpose. I grew up with a deep sense of God in my life, and I never deviated from my belief in Him, except when I started to take the glory for the plans of achieving my goals and my plans. But none of my plans had any longevity. They were built on sand. These experiences made me focus on the reason for my existence and purpose and eventually took me to the center of God's word.

I decided to put aside the money-chasing plans and deal making, and focus on God and the purpose He wanted for me. I started seeking Him through reading His word and attending men's Bible studies and church, while also giving back to the community. God has a way of strengthening you when you are at your weakest point. Indiana was a place where I experienced spiritual growth by developing relationships with men and women of God. When I first moved to Indiana from the Bahamas, I met Forrest Dickerson, who invited me to Greater Northwest Church. He and his family embraced me and provided fertile ground for me to grow in Christ. I was already a Christian but needed a place where I could worship and grow. I later joined Eastern Star Church and became involved in the church by singing in the Men of Standard all-male choir. This was one of the most rewarding experiences I had as a member at Eastern Star. I admired the way that Pastor Jeffrey A. Johnson simply delivered the truth from the word of God and made it plain to understand. I met with Pastor Johnson and shared my vision and the ministry I believed God was calling me to. I started supporting Eastern Star financially and furnished Jewel Christian Academy School with new computers. Pastor Johnson and I became teammates on the church basketball team, and he became a mentor and friend.

I had several negative experiences in my business relationships, but God provided a counterweight and balanced those experiences with the positive ones I experienced at Eastern Star. Jeffrey Johnson was one of those men that God put in my path and life to reinforce the purpose that He wanted to reveal to me. I began to grow spiritually during times when my personal and business life was deteriorating. I realized that God's grace kept me, and the scripture "my grace is sufficient for you, for my power is made perfect in weakness"[192] was a foundational principle that I applied to my faith. This scripture fueled my passion to pursue God, because I knew that I was weak and needed God for strength.

I later joined the YMCA Board of Greater Indianapolis, the Leukemia & Lymphoma Society, the Christian Business Men Committee (CBMC), and other charitable organizations. At CBMC, I met Waite Archer, a Christian businessman, who later mentored me in insurance management and taught me about golf and life. I volunteered to coach and mentor troubled youths through the Big Brother, Big Sister program. I later met Al Fox of Community Youth Connection (CYC) and supported their mission to serve underprivileged students by providing needed food and clothing. I took the focus off myself and focused on the needs of others. Additionally, I worked with Athletes in Action and the Coalition of Christian Athletes and became involved in the Legends of the Hardwood honoring John Wooden, Hall of Fame basketball coach. I met Coach Tony Dungy, former coach of Super Bowl Champions Indianapolis Colts; he brought his son, Jordon, to my son, Zion's, birthday party. He is very personable and is a man of purpose and unwavering faith in God. I appreciated the way he represented himself in the NFL and how he stood on God's principles regardless of the circumstances. I learned a lot from observing his life. I was also able to meet with legendary Coach John Wooden. He shared with me his keys to life, which I still use today.

God has a way of putting men and women in your life to help shape your purpose as they discover and operate in their own. Dr. E. Dewey Smith, another man that God placed in my life, showed me how all of these relationships of purpose had helped shape what God was about to do in my life. I shared with him many struggles that I faced and how each situation and trial had helped shape my perspective first of who God is, and then who I am. He and I shared similar experiences, although my development was in corporate America and his was in ministry. To hear how consistent God is first in the revelation of our purpose and then its development was comforting. In each of our lives, our Creator reveals Himself to us and confirms what we believe He has taught us in His word. He gives us a test, so that we can confirm what we know to pass the test. E. Dewey confirmed that God tested him, his obedience to follow and trust the Creator, no matter what other men, pastors, bishops, or deacons said. And every time he put his trust in God, his faith was tested, and he moved from believing God to knowing God.

So how can we move from a belief in what our purpose is to knowing? First, we have to move from a belief in who God is to the knowledge of Him. I realized that I can only know what "I am" supposed to do in this life by knowing who the "I AM"[193] really is. God is the source of everything, as the psalmist recognizes that the Lord is our Shepherd, and we shall lack nothing. The key here is to also understand that in order to have a shepherd, we must recognize ourselves as sheep. Sheep depend on the guiding hand of the Shepherd, on his rod, and on his staff. They depend on him for guidance, protection, and deliverance in time of trouble. We need the I AM to guide us in the revelation of our purpose.

These Christian men were great examples of what God could do when you put your trust in Him. They were all operating in their purpose, and this started me on a journey to seek God more sincerely and use the relationships that He wanted me to be a part of, as opposed to the ones that I was trying to foster and create on my own. As I look back, it was the purpose in areas to give back that grounded me again. I started seeing through the veil and asked myself how I could help others instead of focusing on myself. I was looking through the wrong lenses in trying to deal with my own inadequacies. The moment that I started focusing on my Creator as opposed to creation, I started cultivating fertile ground for God to manifest His purpose in my life.

I began speaking to youth groups and was asked by a minister to speak at his church, St. John's Missionary Church. How ironic. I attended St. John's University and now I would preach and speak at St. John's Church. I was made nervous by the invitation, but I accepted. I remember the minister's wife telling me that her husband very seldom offered the podium to anyone, especially someone he had just met. I taught a lesson titled "The Dominion Promise" on how God commanded us to have dominion or "to dominate" everything around us, except people. It turned out great, and ever since then, I get a greeting of "Pastor" now and then at a restaurant or out in public. I have accepted other engagements at churches and Bible studies, but have not ventured into that realm completely yet. I guess God's purpose for me in that area is still in hot pursuit.

All of my experiences have led me to do what God called me to do, which is to write this book and to get involved in organizations that give back to the communities they serve. Water World Solutions Foundation is one of those organizations. According to UNICEF, 1.1 billion people lack access to clean, safe drinking water, with 900 million of them living in rural areas that have the potential to be served by mobile systems. Additionally, according to the United Nations, 9500 children die each day from waterborne diseases from contaminated water sources. To address these issues, Water World Solutions has developed the mobile water treatment solution, which is a proprietary process of converting contaminated water into clean drinking water. The treatment produces medical grade, clean, fresh, inexpensive, and, most importantly, safe drinking water through the eradication of bacteria, viruses, algae, spores, cholera, and protozoa—all things unsafe in drinking water. This issue is so serious that I believe the conflict in Africa over oil will change to water some day. According to the United Nations, water will be the single biggest source of conflict and war in Africa in the next twenty-five years. I traveled to India and Africa to design a program with the leaders of the various countries to address this global problem. My plans are now centered in God's purpose for my life, but it was not until I stopped focusing on the wealth of the world and placed my focus on the wonders of His word.

I had many plans for my life, some that did not include God and family, and others that did. My heart had always been set on Him; I just needed to turn up my passion for Him, as He turned up His purpose for me. I went through hardships in my life and am still experiencing some, but I know that God's purpose will prevail, and He will see me through. All I need is a good memory to know that God has patience with our plans and potency in His purpose.

Where are you standing? Are you standing on your plans or on God's purpose? Keep your heart set on Him, and even as you plan, He will work it out for your good. Joseph's brothers plotted his death and eventually sold him to a place where he ended up saving their lives. As a mathematician, I can appreciate the formula "God can add by subtracting." He added to Job's life by subtracting from it. He is the only one who can remove the fruitless trees in our lives, while adding the good trees that allow us to bear good fruit. Commit to the Lord whatever you do, and your plans will succeed.[194] Notice the passage says "whatever" you do. If it is committed to God, it will be meaningful and purposeful. If you keep your heart set on God, He will subtract the bad plans you make and add good plans that He purposed in your life that equate to fulfilling your destiny and purpose.

Chapter Twelve
It Will Endure

☙

"For the Lord is good and his love endures forever; his faithfulness continues through all generations."

PSALM 100:5

"It's about the journey—mine and yours—and the lives we can touch, the legacy we can leave, and the world we can change for the better."

TONY DUNGY

"But the plans of the Lord stand firm forever, the purposes of his heart through all generations."

PSALM 33:11

"The resolution to have your purpose revealed by the Creator will profoundly affect yours and the lives of your children's children. God establishes a purpose through love that survives the possessor and endures so that it will be a blessing to future generations."

RICARDO A. RICHARDSON

We have looked at many people and how purpose has influenced their lives and the lives of future generations. However, each of these individuals, like you and I, had plans of their own and also erred, as humans tend to do. The only one who did not show any faults in his plans or purpose was Jesus. He stood on the side of purpose, and even at imminent death He declared that not His will (desire or plans), but the will (purpose) of the Father be fulfilled.

There is a universal purpose that we all have, which is sharing our experiences and encounters with God with others. God is the one that delivers and saves, and He instructs us to share our testimony with others. We can only give a testimony when we have gone through various tests in life. Jesus paid the ultimate sacrifice to save God's people, all of humanity, as Joseph saved his family from famine and death. God's purpose is to continually reveal itself to humanity so that we are able to tell of His goodness to all generations. It is our responsibility to teach future generations about God and how they are to uncover His purpose for their lives. When God reveals a singular purpose in your life, it is to affect others in your life. The decisions you make affect those around you, even generations of your family.

God warned the people of Israel that they needed to follow his commandments, even if their fathers did not. The issue at hand was that the perverse ways of the father were usually performed by the son, unless a prophet of God or instruction was given to the son. If this continued, God said that He would not bless the generations to come. We are talking specifically about idol worship, but people today worship many idols, including money, fame, power, pride, position, and people. "You shall not bow down to them or worship them; for I, the Lord your God, am a jealous God, punishing the children for the sin of the fathers to the third and fourth generation of those who hate me, but showing love to a thousand generations of those who love me and keep my commandments."[195]

It is clear that we are to remove the veil that causes us to focus on the wrong things in creation. We are to focus on finding knowledge of the Creator, and in so doing we will discover knowledge of self in relation to Him and be able to instruct others in the right way to go. Additionally, you will discover the love and compassion of the Creator. He says for those who love Him He will show love to a thousand generations, or to the nth generation. The Bible says in Psalm 136 that God's love endures forever. God wants to bless you, reveal to you every good thing that He has for you, and will show you His purpose and plan for your life. All He requires is for you to love Him because He first loved you. Paul says, "For I am convinced that neither death nor life, neither angels nor demons, neither the present nor the future, nor any powers, neither height nor depth, nor anything else in all creation, will be able to separate us from the love of God that is in Christ Jesus our Lord."[196]

This is a very powerful statement. The Creator of all things and of all people created you to make a difference in the world. You are the salt that gives the earth flavor. He created you for a purpose, already victorious. Nothing will separate His love from keeping you safe and from connecting you to His kingdom. Only you can separate yourself. How? By not submitting to the Creator, but submitting to those created. If God will connect you to the trees, which provide the oxygen you breathe, surely He will connect you to others to help them breathe and live.

Moses was one of the most powerful characters in Scripture; his decisions affected a generation of people. God chose him to lead the Israelites out of slavery to the promise of a better future, even though Moses was a murderer who killed an Egyptian. Ultimately, Moses led one generation of people out of slavery in Egypt but was not allowed to lead the next generation; that assignment would pass to Joshua. Moses was able to lead Israel out of Egypt, but he was unable to get the mindset of Egypt out of Israel. God wanted to lead a new generation of young warriors to a new place, with a new mindset.

Joshua carried this new mindset and asked the people to choose whom they would serve, because he knew that some of them were worshipping idols and doing things against the law of the commandments that Moses had given them. "But if serving the Lord seems undesirable to you, then choose for yourselves this day whom you will serve, whether the gods your forefathers served beyond the River, or the gods of the Amorites, in whose land you are living. But as for me and my household, we will serve the Lord."[197] Joshua took a stand for God with his generation before his leadership began and affected generations that followed. Even if you have not taken a stand for God and have chosen your own plans, God still wants you to take a stand for Him so He can establish you in this generation. One of the most important gifts that God has given man is the right to decide. We can even decide our own salvation. This day I give you death and life, now you choose. Decide to have your purpose revealed with potency. Decide to seek the Lord of all! Decision is the only thing that gives man an identity. Otherwise, we are drones without a mind! It is your life, not everyone else's! Instead of choosing to have Christ renew their own minds, others have cast their old mindset onto other people! Don't be influenced by these people. Seek the mind of Christ. Set your mind on the fruits of the Creator and on your purpose through Him!

Gideon considered himself a coward, the weakest of his family, who was the weakest of the tribe. Gideon inherited this mindset from those before him. He was taught that he was a weakling, and he developed self-esteem issues and continually needed reassurance and encouragement. I can imagine what Gideon heard as a young boy growing up: "You will never amount to anything in life," "You are weak and afraid," "You are so stupid," "Why can't you be more like your brother or sister," and "You are a coward, just like your father and grandfather." These are statements still made today, crippling words that stay with us for a lifetime and are passed on to our children when we begin to internalize them and speak them into their lives. An African proverb states: A blow passes on, but a spoken word lingers. Unlike a physical bruise, words are able to penetrate your heart, causing internal bruises. This is why God speaks to our hearts and spirits through His word. Solomon states in proverbs: "An anxious heart weighs a man down, but a kind word cheers him up."[198]

No type of abuse should be tolerated, but mental abuse is subtle and deteriorates the mind over time. Words are very powerful tools. Depending on the circumstances and events surrounding them, words can build or tear down a person's character. "Like apples of gold in settings of silver, is a word spoken in right circumstances. Like an earring of gold and an ornament of fine gold is a wise reprover to a listening ear."[199] We can easily see how important words are, as another proverb states, "Pleasant words are like a honeycomb, sweetness to the soul and health to the bones."[200]

Words that we speak to each other can build up or tear down; they can create a healthy self-esteem or a low one. Gideon's self-esteem was so abused that he could not see himself even as his Creator saw him. God changed the generational fear that Gideon possessed and called him a mighty man of valor. The lesson here is that words can uplift, and support confirms the words and encouragement given. You can encourage yourself if no one else does, and the support given will confirm the words of encouragement. God says that you are wonderfully made and He made you a winner, so act like you are one. Speak words of encouragement and love over yourself until they are ingrained in your psyche. When someone calls you stupid or ignorant, say to yourself, "I am made in the image of the Creator, and I have wisdom and knowledge of God and myself."

You cannot accomplish anything until you first believe you are worthy and able. The same holds true for those around you. You can use words to create a more positive culture in your life to replace a toxic one. God used words to create, and whatever He spoke accomplished its purpose. He obviously believed that what He spoke would happen because He is an omnipotent, omniscient God. When we operate in the knowledge of God, we can speak and believe, and it shall come to pass. "So will My word be which goes forth from My mouth; it will not return to Me empty, without accomplishing what I desire, and without succeeding in the matter for which I sent it."[201] The words that the Creator speaks over your life about who you are will encourage and support you all the way through.

I like the way God dealt with Gideon as He saw him through the entire process. He called Gideon to save the tribe against the enemy, even while Gideon was hiding. Then He encouraged Gideon over and over again, building his confidence and self-esteem. Gideon finally began to believe that he was a mighty warrior and started to act like one. Just as Gideon heard from his family and tribe that he was a coward over and over again, God reassured him of his valor and might over and over again, until Gideon started to believe Him. God knew that he needed the words of other men to confirm it, even though God's words are the highest authority. If God can call a weak man like Gideon, along with 300 men who lap the water like dogs, to be His army and give them seemingly impossible victory, then He can do the same in your life. The only words that should matter to you are the ones spoken by your Creator, the same words of encouragement that he spoke to Gideon. They will shape you into what God intended you to be in this generation and you will influence the next generation in knowing the God that influenced you. Gideon had a profound effect on his and future generations because He believed what God called him.

When we discover the thoughts and purpose God has for our lives, our lives should reflect that purpose in our thoughts and actions. A quote often attributed to Dutch theologian Desiderius Erasmus reads, "Watch your thoughts for they become words; watch your words for they become actions; watch your actions for they become habits; watch your habits for they become your character; and watch your character for it becomes your destiny." Your thoughts, both negative and positive, shape who you will become. God spoke to you about His thoughts toward you: "For I know the thoughts that I think toward you, says the Lord, thoughts of peace and not of evil, to give you a future and a hope."[202] What a wonderful promise! This word should cancel out any negative thought anyone has ever had or expressed to you. This is the thought that you should have about yourself, because your Creator has this thought of you. Notice God said I have a thought to "give" you a future and a hope. If we could sum up in one word the theme of this book, it would be "give." God has your purpose, your joy, your happiness, your destiny, and wants to reveal and give them to you. How can we expect to receive a gift from someone we don't have a relationship with? God is your Creator and He is the most important person that you should know. After all, who knows you better? In order for you to develop habits about how you are to function, you have to first have the right thoughts. Your thoughts then will shape your destiny, which will influence future generations.

As we observe the life of Esther, we see that it was not always one of royalty. Esther believed she could be queen even though she was an orphan. Her cousin helped shaped those thoughts into reality. We may go through our orphanage times or times of trouble, difficulty, and struggle, but our thoughts of what God calls us and our purpose will make provision for us to survive until it is ready for the manifestation in our lives. For some, the purpose is revealed while we are still living in the orphanage stage. We may discover that we developed the fortitude in that situation to help others not to fall victim to it, and that our lifestyle is just that, a style of life; it is not our life or the definition of who we are. Esther was a queen even while she was an orphan; everyone else, including King Xerxes, just didn't know it yet. But God did, and He purposed Esther to rule the kingdom and to save her people from destruction.

David was a man after God's own heart, and God called him His friend. David always had a heart for God. He acknowledged God in most things he did, and God gave him victories throughout his life. Although David was living a life of purpose, like you and I, he also had many faults. David lacked discipline toward his children and was unable to provide a functional home for them. He focused on his work and neglected his home life. He had a quick temper, as seen with Nabal, the husband of Abigail. He was going to kill him for not providing food for him and his men. He was unfaithful and plotted to have Uriah killed because he wanted to take his wife, Bathsheba, as his own. All of these were faults because David was a man. Without God, he would continue in these faults, but God delivered him and was a friend to him. David fostered a culture among his later sons that continued through the generations. David was a dedicated and repentant servant of God, and he was forgiven of his many sins and misdeeds. David had his own plans as to how his family would continue, but God had a different purpose. God has a way of stepping in and ensuring that the future generation operates in His purpose. David planned, plotted, and took Bathsheba, the wife of Uriah, so God took the life of their first son.

The second son born of Bathsheba, Solomon, succeeded his father David as king of Israel. Just as David had many faults, so did King Solomon. God showed favor to Solomon and blessed him with wisdom, knowledge, and wealth. Solomon was known for his wisdom, wealth, and writings, composing more than 3000 proverbs and 1005 songs. But he allowed his wives to worship their own gods, and even built shrines for their sacrifices. Later in life, Solomon followed the mindset of the generations before him, worshipping idols and forsaking the teaching of his father and of God. Solomon showed favoritism to the men of Judah and alienated the northern tribes. He placed taxations and heavy burdens on the people that further alienated them and made them bitter. Before he died, his kingdom had been under heavy tension for seven years, causing division among the tribes and people. Like his father, Solomon made plans and decisions that affected his generation adversely. God made a promise to David and blessed his son Solomon, who ultimately affected the next generation of kings. The kings of Israel and Judah rebelled against God, while others served Him. This cycle of rebellion and dedicated service toward God continued for generations that followed.

The reason I am pointing out the faults of so many is that God doesn't expect us to be perfect; in fact, He can use you when you feel useless. God wants us to recognize our flaws so that we understand that He can use us in our flaws.

There is a legend about an elderly lady who had two water jugs, one that was flawed with a crack on the side. The elderly lady traveled slowly to the river to draw water each day. She took the two water jugs with her on her journey, but when she returned home, one was full and the other only had half of the water in it. Each day she walked to the river to draw water and returned, but just as before, the cracked jug would only have half of the water in it. After a long time, the jug, in despair, asked the woman why she did not repair him because he was flawed and only was able to hold half the water. The woman replied by asking him if he saw all the beautiful flowers along the path on her way home. She told him that she had planted seeds along the same path on which she walked home. She explained that if not for him watering the seeds, the flowers would not have grown, and although the other jug was useful to bring a full amount of water home, he was able to bring water and help the beautiful flowers along his path to bloom.

Some of us are flawed like the jug, but God uses our flaws to help others in our path. God refreshes and reforms us with His word and causes us to bloom. We become a living, "flawed," yet perfected testimony to Him that others can see.

Even though we are flawed, as Gideon, David, Solomon, or even the cracked jug, you and I are still valuable to the Creator, because He knows what the flaws are useful for. The pot has no idea of its uses, but the holder of the pot does. Similarly, you and I know of our flaws and limitations, but God knows our purpose and how to use our flaws and limitations to our advantage. Some of the most successful people experience weaknesses, hardships, and character flaws.

At the time I began writing this book, I was experiencing many personal hardships. I went through separation and divorce. Business was very slow, and I was unable to be as mobile as I would like because of lack of adequate transportation. I lost my home, car, and investments, and was walking or riding a bicycle. I rode my bicycle about ten miles each day to meet my son, Zion, at the bus stop. The cars would race by me in sunshine or rain, respecting only other vehicles on the road. At the bus stop, all the other parents would wait in the comfort of their vehicles, while I waited for him in rain or cold weather. I comforted myself that I could wait for him there until his mother picked him up, although the ride home would feel a little bit harder, and in the winter, the wind would cut through my gloves and layers of clothing. I had responsibilities that included paying spousal and child support that took precedent over purchasing an automobile. I now had a different outlook on life from having to adjust to riding a bicycle after driving Mercedes, Porsches, and BMWs. This was the most humbling experience I have had; but it was also the most rewarding. Whenever Zion saw me, he would jump off the bus and run full speed toward me, rain or shine. I would drop my bike and hug him every day, which made the ride worth it.

I had a red backpack that I used to carry my groceries. After several trips to the grocery store (I could only fit a few things in the backpack), I realized that I didn't need the extra packaging, so I would unpack the cereal or other boxed items so that it would all fit in the trunk (backpack) of my bicycle. Whenever I got discouraged about having to ride my bicycle, God reminded me of the strength He gave me to ride my bicycle every day. I was getting in shape physically because of the long uphill rides and the rides against the wind with the additional weight of the backpack on my back. In the trunk of my new car, I still carry that red backpack. Every time I open the trunk, I see it and am reminded of when I did not have transportation. I am reminded of the times that I rode my bicycle to meet my son at the bus stop. I am reminded of how I thanked God that I was healthy enough to ride and was grateful for health. I am reminded to give God thanks for all His blessings, both great and small. Through the process of authoring this book, and fulfilling a purpose, God has blessed me tremendously. All that I have lost when I depended on creation, has been restored and multiplied by my Creator. Because I dug my way to the core, God has revealed my purpose and blessed me through the slices.

I remember reading the inscription on a small piece of wood on the dresser of Emperor Haile Salassie when I visited his private room at his palace in Addis Ababa, Ethiopia. It read: "Every moment overflows with His blessings." That had such a profound impact on my life. Each and every moment that we live and breathe, no matter how sorrowful or joyful, overflows with God's blessing. It is all in your perspective! What an awesome thing! We just have to recognize our hardships as blessings.

Even though Water World Solutions Foundation and I have been diligently working with new technology to deliver mobile water systems to people who need it, red tape and bureaucracy slows the process. It gets very frustrating when you have so many plans and they are slow to materialize. That is when you have to stay connected to the Source. Your purpose and passion will always water and refresh you.

I experienced some hardships that have caused me to reflect on my life, and writing this book has been very therapeutic for me. In fact, my own plans have not materialized, and I have had to lean on God's purpose and plan for my life. My circumstances and burdens are so heavy at times that this book has given me a true sense of purpose. Everything else is out of my control, although true control is an illusion. The writings that began as a need to pass the time and empty my thoughts of hardships have become a need to fulfill a purpose and achieve personal fulfillment. I need to write this, if not for anyone else, for myself. God is pouring in and through me in these pages. I had to be in these circumstances in order to be honest about my situation and where I am in life. I am totally submitted to my Creator and know He is working in strength while I am weak. The Bible says that God's strength is made perfect when we are weak. Many of the words I have written were inspired; I cannot take credit for them. They came from the Creator of man and words.

Again, I never actually thought I would write this book, although the idea of the book was with me for a very long time. I guess that thought of purpose kept nagging at me and pursuing me until I realized I could not avoid it. Remember, our thoughts are the spark that develops words, character, action, and destiny, all defined by purpose. God wants there to be no doubt that He is the inspiration of all we do in His name. He can use you when you don't feel useful, even when you feel like a flawed, cracked jug.

I stood on my plans for a very long time, not God's purpose. When you stand on the side of man's plans, you miss the other side: God's purpose. You can plan, but don't stand on them, for they are built on sand. Don't put your hope in your plans unless they are also the plans of God. Put your hope in God's purpose, and He will make His purpose your plans. Every person of purpose has dealt with men of plans. Some plans are there only to stop your purpose from manifesting, but God uses man's plans for His purpose.

Even as we continue to plan our future and the futures of our children and seek to provide a better life for ourselves and our families, we must realize that God's purpose—as His blessings—is generational. He establishes a purpose that survives the possessor so that it can continue to be a blessing to future generations. An inheritance can be more than just material possessions. It can be words, wisdom, habits, prayer life, or traditions. In fact, many of us have been taught that money is the only inheritance that can be left to our loved ones. Leaving money alone without wisdom or instruction may not be a blessing, but a curse! The Bible says that ruthless men gain only wealth, while gracious ones gain honor.[203] But to gain wisdom is much more desirable than gold, more desirable than wealth. Wisdom should be passed along to help the generation identify how to use wealth and money as a tool, or they can develop a love for it, which can be detrimental.

Most of us can think of a few inherited consequences or habits in our lives; some bad decisions that others made have affected us in a negative way. My father's drug-abuse lifestyle followed me throughout my life. In high school, I recall one of the cafeteria workers taunting me about my life ending up like that of my father's. I love my father, and he is a great musician and pianist, but his making music was constantly interrupted by the times he was abusing drugs. I played the trumpet and was pretty good at it, but I would start and stop as well for lack of interest. This cafeteria worker had drawn comparisons between us and assumed that I would eventually take an interest in drugs as my father had. This was probably one of the biggest motivating factors for me to go to college, as I was determined not to walk in the footsteps that led to drug and substance abuse.

My father is a very humble and compassionate person, but drugs have taken dominion in his life, and he is malfunctioning according to the "dominion promise." I realized that I was not who this lady said I was going to be. Her words had no authority over my life, and I knew this fact while in high school. At that time, the person who had the most influence in my life was my mother, whose words held more meaning than those of anyone else. Don't let any negative words take root in your life. They are the seeds that you do not want to water or cultivate because they will sprout into weeds. The seed you want to water is the seed of faith. Faith unlocks the mysteries of your purpose and accelerates its pursuit.

I was taught that my heavenly Father and Creator is righteous and perfect in every way, and He wants me to strive to be righteous. I am thankful for a mother who instilled in me a desire to make something of myself, which negated anything anyone could say about me because of my father's lifestyle. My mother was my pillar of strength. She gave me wisdom and instilled positive beliefs in me.

For those of us who had absent fathers in our lives, we can rely on our heavenly Father for guidance every day, and as experienced throughout my lifetime, He has never failed me. Trust me, He is real and will reveal whatever you need from Him.

Proverbs says, "A good man leaves an inheritance for his children's children."[204] We should use our purpose to leave an inheritance for future generations. The growth and development of many of us is a result of the prayers, sacrifices, and labors of love of our friends, relatives, guardians, parents, and grandparents. They made it possible for our generation to do what they could not. They made it possible for us to vote and be counted. We owe it to future generations to sacrifice ourselves to make a better world for them to live in. In fact, even the disciples were taught that they could reap what others who preceded them had sowed. Jesus told them,

I tell you now, open your eyes and look to the fields! They are ripe for harvest. Even now the reaper draws his wages; even now he harvests the crop for eternal life, so that the sower and the reaper may be glad together. Thus the saying one sows and another reaps is true. I sent you to reap what you have not worked for. Others have done the hard work, and you have reaped the benefits of their labor.[205]

To be able to reap what others have done is the blessing that can flow to the next generation. What we work for today may not be manifested until the future or in our children's lives. We can reverse any negative decisions that were made before us by trusting in the One who created us and gave us the wisdom to choose life, as Joshua did, in spite of the fact that the generations before him did not. God is speaking to our generation and the next to rise up! God cares about the future generations.

God's healing ministry was not only limited to adults but children as well. God cares about all generations, young and old alike. Jairus' daughter was twelve years old when Jesus healed her. The story recorded that Jesus raised her from the dead.[206] He only allowed Peter, James, and John to enter into the room with Him. The other disciples and all those who gathered to mourn were not allowed to enter the sick room. We need to be mindful of who we let into our "sick" room, the place where we are vulnerable. We should ensure that the people in our inner circle are positive and not negative or toxic, that they can celebrate us in times of victory and sincerely empathize with us in times of suffering. Jesus had a relationship with all His disciples, but He had a special relationship with these three disciples. Peter means "rock," James means "one who supplants or moves into the position of another," and John means "grace." The story explains that when Jesus spoke to the young girl, he said, "tabitha cumi," which means, "Little girl, arise." I believe that God is saying the same thing to the young people and generations that follow. He wants you to arise from dead situations, dead relationships, and dead plans. Many of us believe our plans are etched in stone. We are rigid and comfortable and don't want to be moved. Peter was the illustration of the rock in this story, and Jesus also brought in James (supplant) and John (grace). God is telling us and all future generations to arise from our rigid, rock hard, dead place and be replaced or supplanted with grace. He cares about you and future generations. He wants you to receive your creative purpose, because you can only be fulfilled when your creative purpose is fulfilled, which will equip you to influence generations that follow.

My sincere prayer and desire is that you receive the revelation of your purpose that will change your life and affect future generations. I hope that this book has inspired you to seek God first, give Him your plans, and receive His purpose for your life, which is deep within you. Stand on His purpose, as there is no safer ground. God wants to manifest His thoughts toward you, His desire, His will, and His purpose to you. As you seek Him and seek His purpose for you, meditate on this version of The Serenity Prayer[207] and let it inspire you. It was written by theologian Reinold Niebuhr.

May God grant you the serenity
To accept the things you cannot change
The courage to change the things that you can
And the wisdom to know the difference.

My addition to the prayer for you is:

May God grant you the desire to seek Him
To gain wisdom, knowledge, and understanding
To go deep within yourself to draw out your purpose
And find happiness and contentment in whatever you do
To walk in the everlasting purpose for your life
And profoundly affect future generations to do the same

As a student with a degree in mathematics and statistics, I am amazed by the way God allows numbers to tell a story. I believe He loves math as much as I do. Numbers symbolize many things in the Bible, including perfection, unity, separation, wholeness, and completeness. Look at this illustration. There are a total of 1189 chapters in the Holy Bible. The shortest chapter in the Bible is Psalm 117. The longest chapter in the Bible is Psalm 119; and the center chapter in the Bible is Psalm 118. There are 594 chapters before Psalm 118, and 594 chapters after Psalm 118. The sum of the chapters before and after total 1188. The center verse of the Bible is … you guessed it! Psalm 118, verse 8. It says; "It is better to trust in the Lord than to put confidence in man."[208] Amazing!

How else can we receive the gift of purpose? We have to put all our trust in our Creator to reveal it to us, and no matter how you slice it, it lies in the core! If there is nothing else you received from reading this book other than this verse, you are about to walk in the "center," at the "core," of the promise and purpose of God, your Creator. We need to trust the Lord God with all our heart, mind, and soul. I believe that God was at the center (heart) of this. It you want to know the central purpose of God's will for your life, then go to the center of His word, Psalm 118:8, put all your trust and confidence in Him, and you will discover His perfect will and reap the fruits of your purpose.

You were designed to search and go deeper within yourself to find your purpose. Trust me, it is in there! Purpose is the only reason you exist! God designed you to operate in a personal purpose that is a part of His universal purpose. You have to have a personal relationship with your Creator to receive the true purpose for your life. Before you analyze God, personalize Him, and then you will realize that He alone is potent and sovereign. He created you to seek Him for your purpose. God wants you to seek wisdom, knowledge, and understanding. To seek these things, you need to seek God and His Son, Jesus Christ, the radiance of the Creator's glory. Along the way you will discover and learn all about love, joy, happiness, and contentment, and you will discover your purpose for your life.

It is very simple to search God for your purpose. The first thing you must do is confess that you have trusted creation, your plans, and the plans of others for your life, and that you cannot do this on your own any longer, that you need His guidance in your life. Repent and acknowledge that you cannot do it all by yourself and accept Jesus Christ as your personal savior and purpose guide. Jesus will instruct you to live a purposeful life as He did. Admit that your way has not worked and you want to seek a new and better way. Pray this prayer and believe: God and Creator of all purposes, my way has not worked for me. I have been searching creation instead of seeking you, my Creator. I believe that Jesus Christ, your Son, died for my sins so that I can have a purposeful and everlasting life. I now invite Jesus Christ and the Holy Spirit to come into my heart and life, as you purposed[209] for Him to do. I turn from my life of selfishness and sin and give all my plans to you. I no longer put my confidence in people, but I put my trust in you. Give me your plans and your purpose for my life, so that I may enjoy the fruits of your Spirit. In Jesus' name, amen.

That is all that is needed to activate and accelerate the pursuit of purpose in your life. You no longer have to worry about your purpose or if your life will be meaningful. God will begin to take you on a journey and reveal your purpose to you along the way. Walk with Him through life and watch it unfold. Stay connected to the True Vine, and He will make you a purposeful branch.

You have now begun a new journey in life. You hold the same keys that Joseph, David, Mary, Solomon, Moses, John Wooden, Myles Munroe, Tony Dungy, and many other believers have to unlock and reveal God's purpose and will for your life. Keep living, keep believing, keep loving, and keep learning of God. Don't worry that you have been planning your life to this point and have regrets about the decisions you have made in the past. Wherever you are in life as a result of your plans, just stop, breathe, and accept that your Creator understands the reason of your being alive today and choose to accept Him as the Lord (owner) of your life, and although your plans may or may not have you where you want to be, His purpose will have you exactly where you need to be.

Notes

1 John 14:6a (KJV)

2 Psalm 139:13-15 (NRSV)

3 Isaiah 29:16 (NIV)

4 Revelation 1:11

5 Ecclesiastes 3:1 (KJV)

6 Romans 8:19

7 Ecclesiastes 2:26 (NIV)

8 Ecclesiastes 12:13 (NIV)

9 Matthew 6:33

10 See Genesis 37-50.

11 Genesis 37:10

12 Luke 23:34

13 Jeremiah 27:6 (KJV)

14 Genesis 50:20 (NIV)

15 Romans 8:28 (NIV)

16 Proverbs 19:21 (NIV)

17 Proverbs 20:5 (NIV)

18 Jacques-Yves Cousteau, *The Silent World*, (New York: Ballentine Books, 1977).

19 "The Michael J. Fox Foundation for Parkinson's Research," accessed November 25, 2014, www.michaeljfox.org.

20 Psalm 139:14 (NIV)

21 James 1:5

22 See Hebrews 11:6.

23 See Luke 8:11.

24 See 1 Peter 1:23.

25 See Matthew 4:4.

26 See Hebrews 11:6.

27 1 Timothy 6:12

28 2 Corinthians 12:9 (NLT)

29 See Book of Esther.

30 Isaiah 43:7

31 Proverbs 19:21

32 Matthew 19:26 (NIV)

33 Philippians 4:19

34 Psalm 84:11 (NIV)

35 Proverbs 13:19a (NIV)

36 Proverbs 18:16

37 See Psalm 23:5.

38 Booker T. Washington, *Up From Slavery: An Autobiography* (New York: Doubleday, 1901).

39 "Ashe So Much More Than a Tennis Legend," *The Seattle Times*. April 12, 1992, accessed November 25, 2014,

http://community.seattletimes.nwsource.com/archive/?date=19920412&slug=1485964.

40 Arthur Ashe, *Days of Grace: A Memoir* (New York: Alfred A. Knopf, 1993), 3.

41 Matthew 11:28-30 (AMP)

42 Jeremiah 1:5 (NIV)

43 Jeremiah 1:7-8

44 See Jeremiah 1:6-10.

45 Psalm 139:13-16 (NIV)

46 Lauralee Sherwood, *Human Physiology: From Cells to Systems*. (Pacific Grove: Brooks/Cole, 2001).

47 Charles Linderman, "A Wonderous Tale of a Sperm Tail," *The Oakland Journal* (Fall 2010): XXXXX.

48 See 1 John 4:4.

49 1 John 5:5 (NLT)

50 1 John 2:6 (NLT)

51 Matthew 20:28

52 Colossians 3:23 (NLT)

53 Mark 15:6-15 (NIV)

54 Matthew 16:13-19 (NIV)

55 Matthew 3:17 (KJV)

56 Pat Williams and Jim Denney, *Coach Wooden: The 7 Principles That Shaped His Life and Will Change Yours* (Grand Rapids: Revell, 2011), 26.

57 See Psalm 18:31.

58 Matthew 16:23 (NIV)

59 Acts 2:41

60 See Matthew 19:16-19.

61 Proverbs 25:2 (KJV)

[62] Matthew 13:14-15 (NIV)

[63] See John 15:4.

[64] John 12:32

[65] James 4:2b (NIV)

[66] See James 1:5.

[67] Matthew 7:7-11 (NIV)

[68] Arthur Ashe, *Days of Grace: A Memoir* (New York: Alfred A. Knopf, 1993).

[69] Arthur Ashe, *Days of Grace: A Memoir* (New York: Alfred A. Knopf, 1993), 3.

[70] Mengiste Desta, *Ethiopia's Role in African History* (Addis Ababa: Shama Books, 2007).

[71] See Philippians 2:7 (KJV).

[72] See Philippians 2:9 (ASV).

[73] See John 13:1-12.

[74] 2 Corinthians 5:17 (KJV)

[75] Deuteronomy 28:13 (NIV)

[76] Pierre Teilhard de Chardin, *The Phenomenon of Man* [*Le Phénomène Humain*, 1955], (New York: Harper & Brothers, 1959).

[77] See Galatians 5:25-26.

[78] Hebrews 13:21 (RSV)

[79] See James 1:13.

[80] See John 1.

[81] See Matthew 6:33.

[82] Luke 23:32 (NIV)

[83] See 2 Corinthians 5:7.

[84] See Hebrews 11:6.

[85] Jeremiah 4:22 (NIV)

[86] Jeremiah 3:6-8 (NIV)

[87] Hebrews 11:6 (NIV)

[88] Larry Schwartz, "Michael Jordan Transcends Hoops," ESPN.com, accessed December 3, 2014, https://espn.go.com/sportscentury/features/00016048.html.

[89] Jeremiah 4:22 (NIV)

[90] Psalm 1:1-3

[91] Matthew 7:13-14 (NIV)

[92] RM Morse and DK Flavin, "The definition of alcoholism. The Joint Committee

of the National Council on Alcoholism and Drug Dependence and the American Society of Addiction Medicine to Study the Definition and Criteria for the Diagnosis of Alcoholism," *Journal of the American Medical Association* 268 (1992): 1012-1014.

[93] See Proverbs 9:10.

[94] 2 Timothy 2:15 (AMP)

[95] Jean de La Fontaine, *Fables* (Paris: Pocket, 2002).

[96] Exodus 2:3-10

[97] Exodus 4:10 (NIV)

[98] Exodus 4:11-12 (NIV)

[99] See 1 Samuel 17:32-50.

[100] Ephesians 6:10-17 (NIV)

[101] Luke 4:18 (NLT)

[102] John 10:10

[103] Luke 1:38 (KJV)

[104] See Luke 1:5-7.

[105] Isaiah 46:10

[106] Luke 1:41-45 (NIV)

[107] Psalm 139:14

[108] Joshua 14:6-14 (NIV)

[109] John 16:23-24 (NIV)

[110] James 4:2 (NIV)

[111] Proverbs 20:5 (ESV)

[112] Genesis 1:11-12 (NIV)

[113] Hebrews 1:3 (NIV)

[114] Joel 2:28 (NIV)

[115] John 4:13-14 (NIV)

[116] Isaiah 44:3 (KJV)

[117] Matthew 4:4a NIV

[118] John 15:1-2 (ESV)

[119] John 15:5

[120] Psalm 119:54-55 (NIV)

[121] Tryon Edwards, *The New Dictionary of Thoughts: A Cyclopedia of Quotations*, (Garden City, NY: Hanover House, 1852; The Standard Book Company, 1963), 45.

[122] Alfred Armand Montapert, *Distilled Wisdom* (Englewood Cliffs, NJ: Prentice Hall, 1965), 36.

[123] Robert V. Remini. *Andrew Jackson and the Course of American Freedom, 1822-1832* (New York: Harper & Row, 1981), 443.

[124] Roy P. Basler, ed. *The Collected Works of Abraham Lincoln,* (New Brunswick, NJ: Rutgers University Press, 1953), 382.

[125] Charles E. Jones. *The Books You Read,* (Harrisburg, PA: Executive Books, 1985), 16.

[126] Revelation 10:10 (NIV)

[127] Genesis 1:26-27 (NIV)

[128] Galatians 6:7-8

[129] Genesis 1:28

[130] See Joshua 1:2-6.

[131] Jeremiah 29:11 (NIV)

[132] See Matthew 22:37.

[133] Proverbs 19:21

[134] Deuteronomy 32:35

[135] 1 John 4:4 (NIV)

[136] Galatians 5:22-23

[137] Matthew 7:14-18

[138] Proverbs 18:21

[139] Judges 6:11-18

[140] Judges 6:14

[141] 2 Corinthians 12:9-10 (NIV)

[142] Judges 6:36-40 (NIV)

[143] Judges 7:4 (NIV)

[144] Judges 7:7 (NIV)

[145] Proverbs 14:12

[146] Numbers 23:19 (NIV)

[147] Judges 7:17-22 (NIV)

[148] Nancy Greenleese, "Philadelphia Teacher Has Been Making Poor Black Kids Into Competitive Swimmers for 35 Years," *Voice of America* (2007), accessed November 25, 2014, http://www.voanews.com/content/a-13-2007-06-11-voa32-66561217/555045.html.

[149] Proverbs 19:21 (NIV)

[150] See Jeremiah 29:11.

[151] John Bartlett, *Familiar Quotations*, 10th edition, (Boston: Little, Brown and Company, 1919), no. 9644.

[152] 1 Kings 3:4-15

[153] See 1 Kings 4:29-30.

[154] 1 Kings 9:3 (NIV)

[155] 1 Kings 8:12-21 (NIV)

[156] Suzanne Weyn, *Mr. Magorium's Wonder Emporium: Magical Movie Novel*, Mti edition, (New York: Scholastic Inc, 2007).

[157] Steve and Marjorie Harvey Foundation (www.smharveyfoundation.org).

[158] See Matthew 15:14.

[159] James D. Strong, *Strong's Exhaustive Concordance* (Hampton, Va: Thomas-Nelson, 2008), 238.

[160] Leviticus 11:44 (NLT)

[161] Marcus Aurelius, *Meditations* (Whitefish: Kessinger Publishing, 2004).

[162] Ibid.

[163] "Quotes by James Dean," CMG Worldwide, accessed December 3, 2014, http://www.jamesdean.com/about/quotes.html.

[164] Cynthia Ozick, "What Helen Keller Saw: The making of a writer," *The New Yorker*, June 2003, accessed December 3, 2014, http://www.newyorker.com/magazine/2003/06/16/what-helen-keller-saw.

[165] Proverbs 14:8

[166] See Acts 17:28.

[167] Revelation 22:13 (NIV)

[168] Exodus 3:14 (NIV)

[169] See Luke 12:27.

[170] Proverbs 25:2 (ASV)

[171] Mark 4:9

[172] Isaiah 43:8

[173] Isaiah 1:1

[174] Isaiah 6:5 (NIV)

[175] Vern McLellan, *Wise Words and Quotes. An Intriguing Collection of Popular Quotes by Famous People and Wish Sayings From Scripture* (Carol Stream: Tyndale House Publishers, 1998), 211.

[176] Isaiah 6:9 (NIV)

[177] Matthew 11:25-27a (NIV)

[178] 1 Corinthians 3:19-20

[179] Matthew 13:11-13

[180] Isaiah 6:9-10

[181] Proverbs 19:21

[182] R. Dohahue Peebles, *The Peebles Principle: Tales and Tactics From an Entrepreneur's Life of Winning Deals, Succeeding in Business, and Creating a Fortune From Scratch* (Hoboken: Wiley, 2007).

[183] Dr. Wayne W. Dyer, *The Power of Intention: Learning to Co-Create Your World Your Way* (Carlsbad: Hay House, 2004).

[184] Tufts University, "Pierre Omidyar," *Tufts Now* (December 4, 2014). http://now.tufts.edu/commencement-2011/pierre-omidyar.

[185] 1 Kings 9:3-9

[186] Isaiah 9:6

[187] Matthew 6:24

[188] Psalm 62:10

[189] Matthew 7:24-27

[190] James K. Galbraith and Travis Hale, "Income Distribution and the Information Technology Bubble" (paper presented at the Association of Public Policy Analysis and Management Fall Conference, Atlanta, Georgia, October 28-30, 2004).

[191] "Will dotcom bubble burst again?" *Quad City Business Journal* (2006), accessed November 25, 2014, http://qctimes.com/business/will-dotcom-bubble-burst-again/article_114ea0f5-677a-5487-8f16-de1faca2dddd.html.

[192] 2 Corinthians 12:9

[193] See Exodus 3:14.

[194] See Proverbs 16:3.

[195] Deuteronomy 5:9-10

[196] Romans 8:38-39 (NIV)

[197] Joshua 24:15

[198] Proverbs 12:25

[199] Proverbs 25:11-12 (NASB)

[200] Proverbs 16:24

[201] Isaiah 55:11 (NASB)

[202] Jeremiah 29:11

[203] See Proverbs 11:16b.

[204] Proverbs 13:22a

[205] John 4:35b-38 (NIV)

[206] See Mark 35:35-43.

[207] Reinold Niebuhr, The Serenity Prayer (1943) as recorded in: Elisabeth Sifton, *The Serenity Prayer: Faith and Politics in Times of Peace and War* (New York: WW Norton & Company, 2003).

[208] Psalm 118:8

[209] Romans 5:8